god and mr. gomez

ALSO BY JACK SMITH

How to Win a Pullet Surprise
Jack Smith's L.A.
Spend All Your Kisses Mr. Smith
The Big Orange
Smith on Wry
Three Coins in the Birdbath

god and mr. gomez

jack smith

A GROLIER COMPANY

FRANKLIN WATTS

New York/Toronto/1982

First published by Reader's Digest Press in 1974

Reprinted by Franklin Watts, Inc.
387 Park Avenue South, New York, New York 10016, in 1982

Library of Congress Cataloging in Publication Data

Smith, Jack Clifford, 1916 —
God and Mr. Gomez

1. Baja California (State) — Description and travel.
2. Smith, Jack Clifford 1916 —   I. Title.
F1246.S58   917.2'2 [B]   747165

ISBN: 0-531-09879-6

Printed in the United States of America
5   4   3   2

To Romulo and Delia Gomez

I cannot make the customary disclaimer that the people and events in this work are not real, but merely creatures of the author's imagination. All the people are quite real, including my wife, and especially Romulo Gomez. I could not possibly have invented Mr. Gomez, and it is not fair to deny so unique a man his name. The snakes, dogs, and rodents herein mentioned are also real, and nothing is set forth as having happened that did not happen.

J.S.

CHAPTER ONE

Mr. Gomez, it occurred to me, was a handsome figure as he walked out ahead of us across his land. A warm northwesterly blew off the Pacific and over the seacliff, lightly pressing his khaki pants against his boots and flapping the brim of his Panama hat. His four dogs circled our little group like Indian scouts, rooting in the tumbleweeds for enemies or prey. They seemed hardly more civilized than coyotes, and like most Baja California dogs they were the yellow-brindle color of the Baja earth.

There was a proprietorial grace in Mr. Gomez's gait. It seemed to flow into his limbs from the land itself. It was a good sign, I thought. He had that air of pride and confidence so often seen in a man when he walks a piece of land to which he holds the title. It was a look that Thomas Jefferson must have had when he walked out to survey his acres on a spring day at Monticello.

I was happily unaware of it at the moment, but this aura of proprietorship, so eloquently implicit in Mr. Gomez's every move and gesture, was the best evidence we were ever to have, except for his word itself, that he was indeed the owner of this land.

My wife and I had fallen behind Mr. Gomez, both of us enchanted at the same instant, it seemed, by the amenities of the exact plot of earth onto which we had just happened. We were not inclined to take another step. There was no need. By some form of communication that lay deeper than mere words or an exchange of glances, we both knew that this was where we would build our house.

"You like this lot?" said Mr. Gomez. He had turned and come back toward us and was watching us now from a polite distance, evidently sensing that we had fallen into a spell and must not be approached too closely.

"You have a very nice view from here," I admitted, making it plain, as a matter of courtesy, that I still regarded the land and view as his, not ours.

"Okay," said Mr. Gomez, taking off his hat as if to commemorate the moment, "this is your lot."

The view was truly so pleasant that I was not alarmed by the ring of finality in Mr. Gomez's remark. We stood on a desert terrace between low green mountains and the sea. Below us the surf pounded into the cliffs, bursting against black rock castles and washing back from a moonscape of glittering tidepools. To the north a dark headland reached out to sea, holding within its arm a shining bay. A fisherman's boat, bright green, lay out on the water like a Van Gogh brushstroke. Sea gulls wheeled and dived, and a flight of pelicans glided over the bay in exquisite formation. Shells and pieces of driftwood shone in the coves. All around us the cactus was in red bloom and the maguey plants were higher than our heads, topped by voluptuous purple buds the size of melons.

It was February, but the sky was blue. Tiny white islands lay out in the sea. The air was pure and warm, and vibrant with the cries of gulls and the scent of salt and kelp and something elusive and vaguely primitive. It might have looked exactly like this a million years ago, except for the fishermen's shacks out on the point and the two brick houses of the Americans on the bluffs a quarter of a mile to the south.

"Mr. Gomez," I said, "it doesn't look to me as if you have any lots staked out. It's just raw land."

"Oh, yes," said Mr. Gomez. He swept an arm around him in a half-circle. "This is your lot. Don't worry. You want some stakes, *señor?* I will give you some stakes."

"All right, then," I said, not wanting to trifle with fate. "This is our lot."

My wife and I looked into each other's eyes, tacitly making a lifelong pact, and then turned toward the sea, allowing the view to fix itself on our retinas and in our minds, so that it might sustain us back in Los Angeles in the months to come when the qualms set in.

Less than an hour ago neither of us had ever seen Romulo Gomez in our lives, nor did we expect ever to see him. Now we stood with him amid this desolate alien beauty, bound forever to him in some exciting but uncertain destiny. I wondered how this could have come about.

I had first heard of Gomez from a fellow worker at the newspaper in Los Angeles, a man named Thomson, who had sat down with me one day in the office cafeteria. He said he knew I was a Baja California buff and thought I might be interested in a man named Gomez. I knew Thomson by sight, but we had never talked before except to say hello.

"Gomez?" I said.

Romulo Gomez, he explained, was a Mexican who owned some land on the Pacific coast of Baja, thirty miles or so below Ensenada, and who now was in a position to lease a few building sites to select Americans. I wondered how Thomson happened to know Gomez, and why he was acting as his agent. He and Gomez, he confided, were partners in a Baja copper mine and a pebble business. The copper was still in the ground, there being no capital yet for its removal, but the pebbles were ready to take.

"You're going to sell pebbles?"

"Yes. We've got half a million tons of pebbles on the beach."

Of course, he added, the beach belonged to the Mexican government, to a line seventy-five feet inland from high tide, so it was necessary for Gomez to get permission from the proper authorities before harvesting the pebbles.

"But don't worry," he said. "We won't have any trouble. They're trying to build up the economy down there, you know."

"I know," I said.

Thomson had been right about one thing, at least. I was indeed a Baja buff. In my youth I had been drawn to Baja as my heroes had been drawn to Everest and the Amazon. I had owned a Model T Ford in which I actually intended to set out over the Baja road for La Paz. It was only many years later, in my delayed maturity, that I began to realize what folly this would have been.

The Baja Peninsula is eight hundred miles long, extending southward like a thin dead twig between two seas, but until very recently there was perhaps no geographical region on the continent so little known. The naturalist Joseph Wood Krutch had called it "the forgotten peninsula," cherishing its desolate beauty as an example of what bad roads can do for a country. William Weber Johnson, in his splendid book on Baja, had called it the "indomitable" peninsula, a word that perhaps explained why it was forgotten. "Lower California," my boyhood schoolbooks called it, translating the Spanish *baja* into English; a worthless sliver that had been broken away from the mainland by some cataclysm millions of years ago, and cut off from the United States by treaty at the end of the Mexican war. These two events, one geological, one political, had created the forgotten peninsula and left it, for the most part, in its prehistoric state.

Baja's rediscovery was among the serendipitous results of the American space program. For there it was, front and center, in Apollo 10's magnificent color photograph of the earth. "What's that thing?" asked many Americans, baffled by the long bright piece of land that seemed to dangle from the shoulder of the continent like a broken arm.

Except for the border towns and La Paz, near the tip, it had remained almost untouched by man and machine. But now there was a good modern freeway from Tijuana on the border down to Ensenada, sixty miles south on the beautiful Bahía Todos Santos. Beyond Ensenada, as I remembered, a paved road ran perhaps another fifty miles, and below that point there was nothing but the notorious "Baja 1000"—a road that was not a road, but merely an unmarked track, sometimes a dozen ruts gouged out side by side in the dust, a multiple of equally unpromising choices that had devoured vehicles by the thousands and spit out their bones. There were no signposts, but the Baja 1000 was well marked by the shells of abandoned cars, scattered along the road like dead insects.

For a few tough souls, the expedition could be worth the hardship and the peril. There were pine-covered mountains rising ten thousand feet above two seas; there was the great central desert on which rain might not fall for years on end, but which gave life to flowering cactus plants found nowhere else on earth; there were turquoise coves and white beaches as lovely as any on the Côte d'Azur; alluring islands in a warm gulf teeming with game fish; and finally the cape, where mangoes, bananas, and papayas grew, and hurricanes were not unknown.

I never quite lost the dream of driving Baja, but fortunately the Model T expired before I could put my mad plan into action, or doubtless its remains would have joined the others along the road, along with my own. Then the war came, and marriage and children, and prudence. As our two sons grew we had often spent our brief vacations at Ensenada. But the idea of building a house in Baja had never occurred to me. I knew Americans had built houses at several communities between Tijuana and Ensenada, but they held the land only on short-term leases. It was the law of Mexico that no foreigner could acquire title to any land along the Baja coast, a law that I regarded as wise, and had no wish to circumvent.

So I was surprised to find myself excited by Thomson's story. A house in Baja? It would be a fine adventure, now that our sons were grown and gone. That's what Americans lacked in their affluence, I thought, a sense of personal adventure, of risk. But I was no longer a wild young man with a Model T. I did not think of myself as daft enough to build a house in Mexico on land I could never own. Besides, though I had no reason to distrust either his motives or his judgment, I knew nothing about Thomson. Still his first name was Lincoln. And it's hard to distrust a man named Lincoln. Even so, it was inconceivable that he should draw me into a Mexican land lease with a man named Gomez; especially a man with whom he shared an interest in a non-operating Mexican copper mine and a scheme for the marketing of pebbles from the seashore.

I dismissed Gomez and his land from my mind, except for mentioning the incident that evening at the dinner table with what I supposed was a tone of sufficient levity to cause my wife Denny to dismiss it also from hers.

"Where is this land," she asked, "exactly?"

"Oh, I don't know," I said. "I didn't go into it that far. On the west coast somewhere, I think, below Ensenada."

"*Below* Ensenada?"

"Yes, I think that's what he said. There's nothing down there at all, you know. No electricity. No water. It's a desert. Forget it."

"What was the man's name?" she said.

"Thomson."

"No, the other man. The one who owns the land."

"Gomez. Something Gomez. That's all I remember."

And with that, I imagined the matter was ended. Our paths had fleetingly crossed that of the unknown Mr. Gomez, and then, like speeding meteors in space, we had veered away on our separate orbits, never to meet again.

CHAPTER TWO

It was many months before the name Gomez surfaced in our lives again, and then it was only when the failure of a lesser adventure had left us far from home and aimlessly looking about for something to do with a lost weekend.

One Saturday in February we had driven down to Indio, in the Coachella Valley below Palm Springs, expecting to attend the opening of the annual Indio date festival. We arrived in the afternoon, only to find the grounds empty and the festival plainly in a state of acute unreadiness. We had misread our calendar; it would be two weeks yet before the festival began. More chagrined than disappointed, I pulled into a service station to gas up for the drive back to Los Angeles. But I had not counted on one of the laws of nature: a woman who is packed for a weekend will not go home ahead of time.

"I suppose we could go back to Palm Springs," I said, not very enthusiastically, "and stay at the spa."

"As long as we've come this far, why don't we just drive on down to Ensenada and look at the property."

"What property?" I asked, genuinely mystified.

"The property that's for lease. You know. The property that man told you about."

I was astonished. I had put Thomson and his dubious

enterprises from my mind. It had never occurred to me that Denny would consider for a moment the idea of building a house in Mexico, or would even remember the conversation. Such an undertaking was not only impractical, but hazardous, fraught with physical as well as legal and financial perils. It was not like her. Or was it? A woman is a permanent novelty. Evidently the notion had lain in her mind all those months, dormant but quite capable of coming into flower when the season was auspicious, like the tulip bulbs she kept in a sack in the refrigerator.

Perhaps she was more adventurous than I thought. Surely she had the genes for it. Her mother, when hardly more than a girl, had immigrated from the Pyrenees and crossed North America to a range of mountains in Southern California called the Tehachapis. It was sheep country, and she had been bonded to work in a boarding house for sheepherders. There she met a young man who had come from the Alps, crossing the Atlantic in steerage. They were married and in time moved down the mountain to Bakersfield, a booming oil and agricultural town in California's great San Joaquin Valley, where, like other immigrants from Italy and France, they enriched the community by the production of beautiful girls.

I had met Denny on a blind date when she was still in high school and I was a young reporter on the local daily. After a courtship which I'm afraid I patterned after the characters of F. Scott Fitzgerald, we were married and bought a house. I was twenty-two; she was eighteen, and we were not ready yet to settle down.

I had tasted some adventure, and wanted more. My father had been a promoter, a dreamer. He was then in real estate in Bakersfield, but we had lived in many towns.

I was always the new boy in school. I read Conrad and Maugham and Stevenson, and one year I stayed out of college and went to sea in the merchant marine as a scullion, which is the lowest form of life in a ship's galley. It was mean work, but we had sailed to Hawaii and Samoa, the Fijis and New Zealand and Australia, and one day, swimming in a sunset at Waikiki Beach, I had promised myself that someday I would come back. This would be my home. Denny and I had hardly been married a year when we sold our house and sailed to Honolulu, with something less than $150.

In Honolulu I found a job on the night desk of the *Honolulu Advertiser* and Denny went to work in downtown Honolulu in radio communications. She, too, worked nights, often handling long communications from Tokyo to the local Japanese consul. They were usually in code. So was the one that came on December 6, the day before Pearl Harbor. That night we went to a party that lasted all night long, as most parties did in those days in Hawaii. We were standing in the yard, saying good-bye to our host, in a pink Hawaiian dawn. Then there was a thump and the earth shook. Later we learned that it had been the battleship *Arizona* blowing up.

That night Honolulu was blacked out. I had to go to work and so did Denny. We said good-bye to each other, assuming, as the navy did, that the enemy would be landing that night or in the morning. Our defenses had been shattered.

In time I grew impatient with civilian employment and joined the Marine Corps, and my wife went back to the mainland to wait it out. It was while I was on Iwo Jima, shortly after the landing, that our first son, Curtis, was born. Douglas was born soon after the war ended and I had returned to Los Angeles and the newspaper business.

Now, in the late 1960s, both our sons were gone; Doug a senior at UCLA, Curt in the Air Force. Since they had left the nest, Denny had been working for United Way, which is the charitable fund-raising organization in Los Angeles County. I had been with the *Los Angeles Times* as a reporter and columnist for twenty years. All of that time we had lived, as we do now, in a small house on Mt. Washington, a semi-rustic older part of Los Angeles near the city's center. We have done some remodeling, and in recent years the new skyscrapers downtown have risen over the peak of the hill to give us a view we didn't have before. Though we can see the tip of City Hall from our window, our house stands above a canyon that is thickly vegetated with native scrub, and quite alive with raccoons, opossums, and red fox, among other charming creatures.

Thus, we were neither restless nor uncomfortable. I was fifty, my wife four years less. Retirement was still a long way off. Our life had not been without adventure. Then why, I wondered, would she be interested in driving down to Mexico to look at land?

In the first place, I pointed out to her that setting out for Ensenada from Indio was not logical. Ensenada was no closer to Indio, in driving time, than it was to Los Angeles. We would have to go over the mountains and down through Hemet and over the back country to the San Diego Freeway. Furthermore, I had no real idea where the property was. Thomson had never shown me a map.

"I don't even remember the man's name," I said.

"Gomez," she said. "It was Gomez."

So it was settled. We drove over the mountains and through the back country to the San Diego Freeway and turned south. The freeway soars through downtown San

Diego and Balboa Park and skirts the backbay where the
ghostly gray ships of World War II lie side by side in
mothballs. It is sixteen miles from San Diego to the Mexican border. It was Saturday afternoon, and we slowed to
a crawl in the thickening traffic as we neared the international gate. Americans by the thousands were heading for
a Saturday night in Tijuana. There was no difficulty with
the Mexican border guards. American tourism is consid-
ered the salvation of Baja California; a doubtful proposi-
tion at best. You thread the gate at a very slow speed and
look questioningly into the gimlet eye of a customs man
in olive drab; you see, or imagine you see, a very slight
nod, and you creep on into Mexico.

Tijuana is easily scorned by more sophisticated travel-
ers as a sleazy border town; a dusty trap of bad streets,
girlie joints, pushers, panderers, and venal cops, all sick-
lied over with a shabbiness and poverty that shock Americans only minutes from the prosperous and tidy beach
towns of California's south coast. Yet Tijuana exerts a
magnetic pull on Americans and Mexicans alike, the first
drawn by a taste for something foreign, the other by what
is said to be the highest standard of living in Mexico.
Tijuana claims, perhaps truthfully, to be the most visited
city in the world.

Whatever its shortcomings, however Americanized it
has become, by osmosis, Tijuana unmistakably is in another country. The moment your car clears the gate and
enters that befuddling montage of alien signs, mad traffic,
and pitted streets, you know that you are no longer under
the benign protection of the U.S. Flag. You are in Mexico;
a very foreign land.

We took the road that skirts Tijuana, running west
along the border to the Pacific, where it passes the seaside

bullring and melds into the Ensenada toll road. The toll road is a divided freeway, a sound and artistic piece of engineering, with two lanes going south and two north along the spectacular Pacific coast. The road is edged with indigenous crushed lava of a magenta color, and in the spring there are banks of red and yellow flowers. It cuts through low coastal hills above the ocean, turning away from one stunning seascape only to discover yet another. The toll is collected at three stations, totaling $2.40 for each car going all the way to Ensenada. It is too much money for the local traffic, so the road is never crowded, and driving it on a good day is like flying in a small airplane a hundred feet above the seashore.

Tijuana was no sooner behind us than I felt a pleasant weightlessness, as if the Baja Peninsula had been detached from the continent at the border and was drifting away in this blue sky and silver sea, just as the Spaniards had imagined. My burdens had been left behind on the mainland, and were receding out of sight, out of mind.

"I'd forgotten how good it feels," I said, "once you get away from the border."

"Yes, I was thinking the same thing."

It had been years since our last trip to Ensenada and we were surprised by the beach house colonies and trailer parks mushrooming along the coast. They had such names as Baja Malibu and San Antonio Shores, and it was obvious that Baja had been discovered by a new wave of Americans; not the hardy lovers of the wilderness, but the affluent ones who wanted to get away, though not too far, and in comfort. The dam was busted; the boom was on.

It was dark when we reached Ensenada. It would have

been folly on top of folly to set off in the night for the perhaps illusionary Mr. Gomez and his illusionary land. We stopped at a new motel, a TraveLodge built and furnished in authentic, or at least convincing, Mexican style. We had a dinner of abalone and white wine at El Rey Sol, a justly celebrated restaurant of French and Mexican cuisine, and took a walk around the town.

Ensenada had grown; it seemed to be experiencing some slow explosion. There were more Americans than ever, and all younger than ever. There were more leather shops and curio stands along the Calle Primera, more dark bars from which came exuberantly sad music, not of the jukebox, thank God, but of live mariachi, the Mexican strolling bands. Not all was lost.

Except for Calle Primera and a few of the other most important thoroughfares, the streets were still unpaved, stony, and potholed. But there was a broad new concrete esplanade down along the graceful crescent shore of the Bahía Todos Santos. Fishing boats and freighters lay quiet at their moorings in the light of a lopsided moon; a gray gunboat of the Mexican navy stood in its dock, and out in the bay a streamlined, white Italian luxury liner lay at anchor, doubtless stopping overnight on a festive cruise from Los Angeles to Acapulco.

For all its growth and lustiness, Ensenada had not yet been corrupted thoroughly into the tinsel and cynicism, the hard bordertown wickedness of Tijuana. It was emerging from the torpor of its neglected past, and it was evidently in a hurry. Soon enough, everyone said, there would be a paved road all the way down the peninsula to La Paz. The engineers had already started on it, working toward each other from either end. Ensenada would then enter the modern world of freeway hustle and prosperity.

For that, I could wait. Meanwhile, Ensenada had stood up to the American impact without losing all its manners and its charm.

In the morning we were awakened early by the roosters of the town. I could awaken in a shuttered room on a Sunday morning in Ensenada and know where I was from the sounds alone. At first light the roosters crow; first one tentative voice, then another, and finally the entire town is aroused and crowing. Then the bells begin to ring in the unfinished cathedral, and finally the radios come on in every house and hovel, crowding the morning air with a chaos of lively Mexican music and commercials delivered in rapid-fire Spanish like bulletins of disaster.

We gave up trying to sleep at the third wave of sound. We checked out and headed south over the road to Santo Tomás. From Thomson's directions I remembered only that to find Gomez you drove into the Santo Tomás Valley and took a dirt road west to the sea, to a place called La Bocana, "the mouth of the river." There you would find Gomez's fishing camp and store.

South of Ensenada the paved road runs straight for ten miles to the farming center of Maneadero. We found the town already astir with Sunday morning life. The fruit stands were open by the road and the vendors were out with their pushcarts. Families in their Sunday clothes walked over the caked mud at the edge of the road toward the small blue plaster church whose solitary bell was calling the town to mass.

Beyond Maneadero the road climbs through low mountains, passing neat little ranches with good adobe houses and shepherds with their dogs and flocks, and then it emerges suddenly on a precipice above the Santo Tomás Valley. We had never seen the valley so green. In fact, we had never been this far south except in summer, when Baja is brown. Now the valley was a Shangri-la of grain fields and bright vineyards in the cup of the mountains. Two centuries ago the padres had built a mission in this valley, and then moved on into history, leaving the diseased and starving Indians behind them, among withering vines and crumbling adobe walls. Santo Tomás was only a village now; a few adobes and a store, and there was said to be a telephone. Only a trace remained, we had heard, of the mission.

We descended a grapevine road into the valley. Two miles before we reached the village we passed a dirt road that ran off to the west, but it looked so unpromising I ignored it, hoping for something better. Once in the village we turned back. There appeared to be no alternative to the road we had passed.

We crossed a rickety cattleguard and then the road struck out through fields of corn and melons and alfalfa planted in a river valley that soon narrowed between precipitous bluffs. The road was unexpectedly good, at first; wide enough for two cars to pass and recently graded. The little valley was an *ejido,* a communal farmland, and we drove past small adobe farmhouses surrounded by broken-down old cars and rusting machinery and galvanized washtubs, and past a one-room schoolhouse painted a faded blue and yellow. There were two outhouses, and a swing and a teeter-totter in the yard.

Subtly the road began to deteriorate, but it was alive. Whole families of pigs rooted in the scrub. Horses and colts romped in meadows among oaks and sycamores, and cows had to be honked out of the roadway. Every few moments, it seemed, I hit the brake or jerked the wheel to avoid a squirrel or rabbit. There were crows, and I saw a hawk circling, and a dead snake in the road. I wondered if it was a rattler.

The houses stood back from the road in the shade of old trees. Women's faces looked out at us from unglazed windows. It being Sunday, the men were out in the yards in their white shirts and good pants, drinking beer from cans and talking and laughing. Children played among the pigs and chickens and dogs, industriously soiling their Sunday best.

The road seemed blocked by low mountains ahead, but the valley flowed through the passes and at last, nearly an hour after we had turned off the paved road, the last peak fell behind us; the road ran beside a grove of oaks and passed through a gate, inside which stood a small whitewashed adobe. There was a great eucalyptus tree towering above the adobe, and a cluster of casuarinas, a tough, pinelike tree often seen on near-desert landscapes or as a screen against the ocean wind. There was a lagoon full of tules and cattails and beyond it the Pacific tumbled up on a crescent beach. We had reached the place called La Bocana.

It wasn't much. The main building appeared to be the little white adobe. In Spanish, I remembered, *la boca* means "the mouth." This was the mouth of the river that had long ago carved the valley through which we had just driven. The river was dry, or perhaps the farmers in the valley had drained it for their crops, but evidently it ran abundantly underground and surfaced here at La Bocana in the lagoon that lay between the adobe and the beach.

The adobe was not as large, I guessed, as our two-car garage at home. It stood at nearly sea level in the riverbed. To the south there was a green marsh running a quarter of a mile to the bluffs of the canyon. To the north there was a hill on which some other buildings stood. There were two weathered log cabins, hardly more than shacks. A third, made of wood siding, was freshly painted and there were curtains in the window. Nearby, on the highest point, stood a small new cabin of brick. There was a scatter of machinery and old vehicles, the usual symbols of wealth in Baja.

It was no more than a hundred yards to the beach. There was a rocky point where the bluffs to the north intruded on the sea, and from there to the southern end of the river's mouth the beach was flat and broad. Two old wooden fishing boats, one a scabrous green, one blue, had been pulled up on the sand from the surf.

Two lean brindle dogs lay in the open doorway of the adobe and a boy sat on a bench outside drinking an orange pop. There was no sign, not even the ubiquitous Pepsi-Cola. I didn't know the building was a store until I peered into the windowless interior and saw a counter and rows of tinned goods on the shelves behind it. I stepped in. The room was unoccupied except for a girl who was sweeping the floor; a girl of fifteen, perhaps, with ivory skin and beautiful large dark eyes. She saw me in the doorway.

"Momento," she said. She leaned her broom against the wall and vanished through a door into a back room that appeared to be even smaller than the one in which I stood.

I waited. There were cases of Mexican beer and Santo Tomás wine. The shelves were full of Campbell's soup, beans, chiles, chocolate, and other staples. If need be, I decided, the place could sustain life. There was a hideous stingray hanging on one wall. It had been preserved in some way and I took it to be an ornament.

There was an aroma to the place, a smell of chiles and corn tortillas and fresh fish, and if I was not mistaken, the tang of tequila, and in a moment a man came out from the back room. He wore khaki pants, a plaid shirt, and a khaki windbreaker. A Panama hat was pushed up on his forehead.

"Buenos días," he said.

"Buenos días," I said, exhausting my Spanish. "Do you happen to know," I asked, feeling a bit foolish, "of a man named Gomez, who has some land to lease?"

He smiled; a smile that showed good white teeth and crinkled the corners of his eyes.

"I am Gomez," he said.

CHAPTER THREE

That was the way we had found him that first day, and we had no more than drunk a bottle of his beer, to wash away the dust of the road, when we had gone with him in his pickup truck, his four dogs running along beside, to look for the first time at the property and make that fateful decision.

Strictly speaking, I suppose, La Bocana would refer to the store and its nearby structures, and to the mouth of the river. But Gomez owns the land for a mile and a half to the north, and calls his entire domain Bocana.

From the store, that first day, we had climbed a steep hill and followed the dirt road that serpentines around it, above the sea. Suddenly we reached the northern end of the hill and a narrow plateau or marine terrace stretched out below us. The land ended in cliffs that rose and fell in height, sometimes soaring to what appeared to be eighty or a hundred feet above the rugged shore. Back of the cliffs the land rose swiftly, away from the sea, into low hills that were then green but would soon be brown.

There were only two houses, both standing on rocky points above the sea, one belonging to a couple named Millard, said Gomez, the other to a couple named Luczynski. They were Americans from Los Angeles. Neither the

Millards nor the Luczynskis had come down that weekend, but Gomez had keys, as a matter of security, and he let us in to see the houses.

The Millard house was pink stucco over brick, with a red tile roof. It had a handsome porch of arches, the width of the house, facing the sea. Inside, the walls had not been stuccoed or painted, and had the pleasing texture of the ocher-colored Mexican brick. Heavy wood beams and rafters supported a vaulted ceiling. The kitchen was dazzling with Mexican ceramic tile. Oil paintings hung on the walls, and I noted they were signed Millard.

Gordon Millard was an executive in a canned goods company, Gomez told us, but he painted when he came to Baja. His wife Opal was a potter, and they had added a studio and a kiln. Their work gave a personal quality to the house. In the clear daylight the colors were brilliant. There was a pervasive aroma of candles and spices. This was a home.

The Luczynskis had not stuccoed their house, leaving it the natural color of the brick. It was smaller than the Millard house, but situated on a promontory that gave it a view down into deep rocky coves on either side. The interior had been painted white, which reflected the light from sky and sea and heightened every color. Art Luczynski too had been dabbling with paint and brush and the walls were ornamented with his playful work.

Perhaps looking into the houses of those people who were to become our neighbors that first day had dissipated the sense of isolation. Except for the scar of the road and the shacks on the point of Santo Tomás two miles to the north, there were only the two houses to show that man had come this way. But there was an ambience in those houses, something almost tangible, like the smell

of tangerines and candlewax. There was warmth and hu-
manness here, and we knew we would not be lonely.

Thus, when we drove on to look at the rest of the land,
we had already been seduced, and when Gomez drove us
back to the store we needed no persuasion. Nothing remained but the routine of a preliminary agreement, and
the sealing of it, perhaps, with a drink of tequila.

He led us into the kitchen at the back of the store,
where a woman he introduced as his wife Delia was cooking something so appetizing that I remembered we **had**
gone without our breakfast. The vapors escaping from the
pans simmering on her butane range were savory beyond
resisting. Surely, I thought, I had never been so famished.

"You have not had your breakfast?" said Mrs. Gomez,
recognizing the stark look of hunger that must have shone
in Denny's eyes as well as my own.

"It's nothing," I assured her. "We'll soon be back in
Ensenada."

"No," she said, "you will have your breakfast with us."

Gomez had taken a half-gallon jug of tequila from a
cupboard and sliced two limes and set the jug and the
limes on the table with a shaker of salt. He poured tequila
into paper cups. It is one of the world's great spirits,
tequila, a clear or light gold intoxicant distilled from the
Mexican mescal plant, a species of which we had seen so
extravagantly in bloom on the land we had chosen.

"After you, *señor,*" said Gomez. His voice was gentle
and slightly musical, with an undertone of humor. There
was a natural grace, I had noticed, in his manner; a polite-
ness that was neither servile nor ironic. Mr. Gomez was,
in fact, a man of such elusive charm, I was soon enough
to learn, that at moments he could be exasperating.

"I'm not sure I remember how it's done," I said.

"Whatever is your pleasure," said Gomez.

I licked the hollow of my left hand between thumb and forefinger and sprinkled it with salt, bit into half a lime, raised my cup and shot its contents back over my tongue, then licked the salt.

"Was that right?" I asked, as a benign internal fire began to warm me.

"*Sí, señor,*" said Gomez, raising his cup. But I noticed that first he took the salt, then the tequila, and last the lime.

Denny also decided to take part in this purifying rite, though Mrs. Gomez elected to stand apart, and then the three of us had another. By the time Mrs. Gomez's succulent preparations had been transferred from stove to table the Smiths of Los Angeles and La Bocana were in a state of euphoria, which nagging questions about the realities of our imminent adventure were unable to dispel.

The meal Mrs. Gomez set before us consisted of burritos filled with spiced ground beef and egg, fried rock cod fresh from the sea, buttered tortillas, beans, and beer, which in Mexico is called *cerveza,* and which is as good as any other in the world. Even without the tequila, I would have recognized it as one of the great breakfasts of my life.

"There is no electricity?" my wife asked over the coffee, getting us back at last to the business that had brought us together.

"Oh, no," said Gomez casually, "there is no electricity. But of course you can have a generator."

"Yes, of course," I said. Generator, it occurred to me, was one of the few words that Gomez had given a Spanish pronunciation, the initial letter having the softer sound of an *h* or *y.* There was a lilt in his English, and a taint of American slang, but it was very good idiom indeed, I thought, for a man who ran a little fishing camp down here a hundred miles or more below the border. Whatever he was, Gomez was not a rustic.

Meanwhile, he pointed out, we could get by on Coleman lanterns for light and when the house was finished we could install a gas range and a water heater and an old Servel gas refrigerator, which surely could be found somewhere, and Gomez would provide the butane for their use.

"What about water?" I asked, knowing there was precious little of it in Baja.

"You don't have to worry," said Gomez. "I will provide the water."

"Where does the water come from?"

"The water, it comes from the reservoir," said Gomez. He had built a concrete reservoir up on the hill above the two houses of the other Americans, and he would, of course, lay pipes down from the reservoir to our house also.

"But where does the water come from," I asked, "that is in the reservoir?"

"From the well."

"You have a well?"

"Oh, yes." That seemed to be his standard phrase for dealing with anxious questions—"Oh, yes," spoken like two musical notes, the *oh* rather high and the *yes* lower on the scale, and full of reassurance.

"Where is the well?"

"It is right here, of course, behind the store."

The phrase "of course" was also a favorite of Gomez's, I had noticed, sometimes having the effect of making the most patent improbabilities seem perfectly credible.

"Where does the water in the well come from?" I asked.

"The water," said Gomez, "it comes from God." It might have sounded pious, but there was a flash of humor in his eyes, and I sensed that nothing was to be gained by pursuing the water to its source at this moment.

I wondered who Gomez really was. We had another tequila with our coffee and he told us a little. He is not a garrulous man; the details were sparse, and much, certainly, was left out. As a boy of fifteen he had left his native town near Guadalajara, in the state of Jalisco, and gone to San Francisco.

"I worked in a mattress factory," he said, "and I went to night school."

But he was a musician at heart and he had left San Francisco and gone to Mexico City, where he organized a band of strolling musicians, the kind called mariachi. They traveled, and finally they came to Tijuana.

"It was the first mariachi band in Baja," he said.

It was in Tijuana that he had met Delia. She had gone to school across the border in Arizona, and like Gomez, spoke English well. Delia Gomez had obviously been a rare beauty, and was now a handsome woman of middle years, with short black hair, bronze skin, and dark mischievous eyes. As she listened to her husband she seemed always on the verge of laughter.

The life of a musician in Tijuana had not been promising for a married man, and during World War II Gomez had engaged in the export of lobster and abalone to the United States.

"I shipped millions of tons," he said. "It was my contribution to the war effort." This boast was not without irony as I reflected that during my years in the service, none of Mr. Gomez's contribution ever reached my plate.

The Bahía de Santo Tomás was one of the bays from which his catch had come, and that was how he discovered his land and bought it, in time, from the government. Some years after the war, the exporting business had been nationalized, squeezing him out, and he had managed ever since to coax a living from his land and the sea.

The Gomezes had a house in Tijuana, where they had raised their four children. The youngest was the girl I had seen that morning in the store, Marisa. There were Sergio and Pepe, both out of high school now, and an older son who was married and had given them four grandchildren. Tijuana was the headquarters for Gomez's enterprises, whatever they were, including the inoperative copper mine and the prospective pebble business.

For a quarter of a century, though, they had spent half of every week at Bocana, tending the store, renting their cabins and camping sites, and supplying the minimum needs and amenities for campers and fishermen. Sergio and Pepe took turns running the camp when their father was away. It was understood that someday the land and the business would be theirs.

When Romulo and Delia were at Bocana they lived up on the hill in one of the pine log cabins, but her domain was the little kitchen at the back of the store. It was perhaps eighteen feet long, but only six or eight feet wide. There were two old gas refrigerators, one stocked with soda pop for the patrons of the store, and an old enameled range. There was a narrow table against the opposite wall, covered with oilcloth. It had a three-tiered wrought iron fruit basket at one end, filled with oranges, lemons, tomatoes, and papayas. Here Delia Gomez fed not only the members of her family, but some of Gomez's workmen, and visitors like us.

As the tequila warmed me after our breakfast in the kitchen I began to expatiate about the house we would build. We wanted nothing elaborate, I told Gomez; surely nothing as large and expensive as the houses of our neighbors. They were beautiful indeed, but we couldn't afford that type of construction.

"What we have in mind," I said, preempting whatever thoughts my wife might have had, "is something inexpensive. We aren't going to *live* down here. We'll just come down on weekends now and then. All we need is a small beach house of American-type construction. You know. Just a frame of two-by-fours with lath and plaster walls and an asphalt composition roof, the kind of thing we'd build in Los Angeles. I'm thinking of maybe eight thousand dollars, at the most."

Gomez shook his head. He knew us already, he said, and we would want nothing less than a house of good Mexican brick and tile, built by himself and his crew. Surely, once we were in our house, we would not want some other Americans to come along and build some little house of sticks and cardboard beside our mansion. And we must think of the land; of the beauty and dignity of the land. It had belonged to Gomez for twenty-five years, a quarter of a century, and he was honor bound to shield it from the desecration of inferior materials and shabby workmanship.

"Very well then," I said, surprised at how easily I agreed. I was not persuaded; I was hypnotized. Our house must certainly be of honest Mexican materials that came up from the good adobe earth of Baja; it would be put together brick by brick by Mexican craftsmen in the employ of Gomez himself. We would do nothing to embarrass the landscape or its owner.

"But there will be no arched porch," I said. "No arched porch. And we can't go above ten thousand dollars. You'll have to keep it down to that. We're not rich Americans, you know."

"You will have a mansion," said Gomez.

"You *do* own the land, Mr. Gomez?" I asked suddenly. It was an extremely impolite question, I knew, but there were so many tales of clouded titles in Baja, and Americans were always uneasy when they built on foreign soil.

"Of course," said Gomez, "I own the land." For the first time I caught the steel in his voice, behind the smiling eyes. "For twenty-five years I have owned this land."

Right then I would like to have seen some authenticating document; a deed or conveyance or an entry in a recorder's register. In the United States, you would have had a title search, and a policy of title insurance, and you would feel secure. No such proof was offered here, if, in fact, it existed. But by now I had no wish to offend Gomez. It had become clear to me that we had entered into some kind of trust, and that we must henceforth proceed on faith, or we could not proceed at all. In any case, later on I would find someone to recommend a reliable attorney in Tijuana or Ensenada and have the title searched. Faith was a fine thing, but you couldn't build a house on it.

Meanwhile, I wanted to secure the site we had picked out. With dismay I imagined it being snatched away from us by some other American couple with an eye for landscape and perspective.

Gomez explained the conditions. He was bound by the law, which, of course, neither of us wished to break. We could not buy the land. The government, in its wisdom, wished to preserve the land for Mexicans. We could only lease it, and for ten-year periods. But Gomez would give us the option of leasing it for successive ten-year periods for as long as we might desire, and our sons after us, on his word.

"Then," I said, "if we lease the land and build a house, the house will always be ours?"

"Of course," said Gomez.

Gomez would send us a contract for the lease. We could sign it and then we would arrange to meet one day in Ensenada and have it properly recorded. I was relieved to learn that at one point along the way, at least, our negotiations were to receive some official documentation.

There remained but one detail. Gomez, I suggested, would like some money; a token of good faith. After all, we might not get back to La Bocana for weeks, or even months, such were the difficulties of extricating ourselves from the machinery of the city; and we couldn't expect our landlord to keep our lot indefinitely from the interlopers who would doubtless soon be at our traces.

"Would a hundred dollars be all right?" I asked.

Gomez shrugged and gave us a deprecatory smile, as if money was not really a material matter in our relationship. Money, in fact, I was to learn, was a subject that Gomez never brought up first, no matter how much of it, in the long run, was to pass from our hands into his.

Denny wrote the check with a hand that betrayed none of the nervousness I felt. She handed it over to Gomez, who slipped it into his wallet without a glance. We were embarked.

We said good-bye to the Gomezes as if they were old friends, and got into our car for the arduous journey home.

"You take care of our lot now, Mr. Gomez," said Denny.

"Of course," said Gomez. "Don't worry. *Vaya con Dios.*"

We were oblivious of the hours as we drove home through the clouds of our own fantasies. We were building our house with conversation, and it was indeed a mansion.

CHAPTER FOUR

For weeks our fever raged on. We drew a dozen house plans and I brought home a pile of books from the library on building beach houses or desert hideaways. Our fancies raced beyond the house itself and into the questions of furniture and curtains and how many guests we ought to invite on a given weekend. I haunted Sears Roebuck to learn about generators and butane appliances, and we scouted around for an old Servel refrigerator long before the foundations were laid for the kitchen it would stand in. Denny began planning the garden. There was to be a row of oleanders between the house and the road.

Inevitably we had our moments of misgiving. Once she was thumbing through a woman's magazine and came to an article called "First Things First," about things one ought to check into before building a vacation house. We had gone beyond the point where we were interested in anything that might dissuade us, but she began reading from the article aloud.

" 'Isolated, remote sites may have their charms, but what about utilities—sewer, gas, water, electricity, telephone lines?' "

I laughed. "We don't score too well on that one," I admitted. There weren't any sewer lines at Bocana, or gas or electricity or telephone lines, either.

"When you get away," I pointed out, "you have to give up something. Who needs a telephone? That's what we're trying to escape."

" 'What about garbage disposal?' " she said, reading from the book again.

I hadn't thought about garbage disposal. With no sewer and no electricity, we couldn't have a garbage disposer. I pointed out that we could keep pigs, like the farmers in the valley. "Or maybe the sea gulls will help us out."

" 'Is the property accessible in winter?' "

"What winter?" All the same, there would be rain, I supposed. There would have had to be some rain for the valley to be so green, and for Gomez to have a well. That dirt road might be an impassable quagmire.

" 'What about interior climatization?' " she read.

"What's that?"

" 'If you overlook the heating problem,' it says, 'even if you are just building a summer cabin, you'll be sorry.' "

"We'll have a fireplace."

"A fireplace? Isn't that new?"

"I just put it in. I don't know why I didn't think of it before. What's a house without a fireplace?"

" 'Where is the closest airport or airstrip?' "

"An airstrip," I pointed out, "is one thing we do have." There was an airstrip on the plateau a mile below Bocana, I had heard. It was a dirt strip, but good enough for a DC–3 to land on. It had been built during the war, according to legend, for use by smugglers of one kind or another, or perhaps for secret military missions.

" 'Is the property free of any bonded indebtedness?' "

"Some things," I said, "are better left unknown. If we

start poking around we'll never build a house."

She put down the magazine.

"Is that all?" I asked.

"What about water?"

"The water," I said, "will be provided by God and Mr. Gomez."

Eager as we were, we resisted the impulse to run down to Bocana every weekend. At this stage it was in Los Angeles at our grindstones that we could best serve the project. Our lot would stay where it was. In a month or two we paid the balance on the lease and began saving toward the cost of the actual construction. No loan would be available. I suspected the very suggestion would ruin an American banker's day. Gomez would have to be paid as he went along, and we didn't want to run short in the middle of the job and create another of those forlorn half-finished dreams that are so familiar on the Baja landscape.

Gomez was ready to commence when we were. His little crew of four were idle—his brickmen and his carpenter and his tile man, who were also his concrete men and his electricians, his plumbers and his roofers. They had drifted back to Ensenada and into God-knew-what temptations after he had finished the last of the two houses. The land waited for its new ornament, which was to be our mansion, as he called it, and Gomez's masterpiece.

It was summer before we got down to Bocana again, just to see our lot once more and to reassure ourselves that a man named Gomez indeed existed in the flesh. Our faith had flagged a bit. It would be restored by the land itself.

It was perhaps more than chance that we pulled up in

front of Gomez's store at lunchtime. Our protests were silenced by the aromas from the kitchen, and we soon were seated at the little table, feasting on chiles rellenos and fried fish.

After lunch we got into Gomez's pickup and he drove us over to the plateau where we had left our lot. My pulse quickened as we topped a rise and suddenly saw the almost-forgotten land. We drove past the Millard house and the Luczynski house and came to a stop at a high point on the road. Gomez got out and we followed, but I felt that something was awry. Our lot, as I remembered, was two or three hundred yards farther on, and closer to the sea.

Gomez walked away from the truck and stood among the tumbleweed and cactus, looking out at the Bahía Santo Tomás. "You see," he said, turning toward us, "you have the most beautiful view."

"This isn't the place," Denny said quietly, her voice out of Gomez's hearing in the wind.

"I know," I said. I turned to face Gomez. "Romulo," I said, for by now we were on first-name terms, "this isn't our lot."

"Why, yes, of course," said Gomez, "this is your lot."

"No. We're both quite sure. It is not our lot."

"Where is your lot?"

"We're down there on that point, much nearer the edge of the bluff, just above those rock castles."

Gomez looked where I was pointing. "You want your house down there, Jack? Okay. That is your lot. But you aren't going to have so beautiful a view."

"That may be so," I conceded, "but this isn't the place we picked out and paid for. It just isn't ours."

It wasn't that there was anything wrong with the new lot, I explained. It did indeed have a beautiful view. It was higher, for one thing, and had a sweeping command of the entire bay from Punta Santo Tomás on the north to the headland south of Bocana. But it made me uneasy, a lot that moved. In the United States, I said, when you bought a lot it had a number and a precise geographical description, and it stayed where it was.

"Jack," said Gomez, "when you build your mansion on this lot, it will not move."

"You know, he may be right," Denny said. "I think it *is* a better view."

"All right," I said, "this is our lot."

It was the first of many decisions that seemed to be our own, but really belonged to Gomez.

The visit to our roving lot sustained us through the summer, and it was September before we could get down to Baja on a weekday to record the lease. Labor Day was a holiday in the United States, but it would be business as usual in Ensenada, where the business was to be done. We would drive down to Bocana and take care of the lease on the way back.

It was late Saturday afternoon when we reached Ensenada, and every habitable motel room in town was occupied. We had planned to stay the night and continue on to Bocana in the morning, not being ready yet to challenge the dirt road in the dark.

"Why don't we go on to El Palomar?" Denny suggested.

We remembered El Palomar from one of our summers in Baja years before. It was a quaint little outpost; a combination curio store, grocery, restaurant, and motel beside the paved road half a mile north of the village of Santo

Tomás. On Saturday nights it was a lively spot, but it was frequented more by the locals than by Americans. The motel consisted of only a few rooms over the store, and most of them were usually vacant.

There was still some daylight when we reached this oasis. We were in luck. The proprietor, a Mr. Villareal, showed us upstairs to our room and told us that the chiles rellenos were very good in the little restaurant below.

I raised the blinds in the room and looked out over the valley. Just across the road, I remembered, though it was hidden in a grove of olive trees, was a beer garden with a swimming pool, rustic outdoor bar, and open-air dance-floor.

Beyond this grotto the valley stretched out to the surrounding mountains. It was green with vineyards that had first been planted by the padres, and from which now came many of the grapes for the premier wine of Mexico —Misión de Santo Tomás.

"Ah," I sighed, "we're really lucky we couldn't find a place in Ensenada, with all those noisy Americans falling out the windows. We'll have a quiet night here."

I should have been forewarned when I went down to the grocery to buy some beer. Two American boys were buying fireworks. These cursed explosives are not merely legal in Mexico, they are the third national sport, after bullfighting and soccer. The boys left with a sackful of firecrackers the size of cigars; big enough, I guessed, to blow the lid off a garbage can, if not the roof off a house.

But I had forgotten the firecrackers by the time we went down to the restaurant for dinner. It was a bucolic setting, dimly lit by candles and an electric light globe which was energized, evidently, by the generator whose muffled clatter we could hear. The waitress moved with the grace and quiet of the jaguar. Either she spoke no English or chose not to waste words. We ordered from a handwritten menu. *"Gracias,"* she whispered, and vanished into the kitchen.

She brought us soup, enchiladas, tamales, and the chiles rellenos, which are green peppers stuffed with cheese, fried in a light batter and served in a light tomato broth. Mr. Villareal had been right; they were indeed delicious. We drank a bottle of Santo Tomás Mosele, observing that the Mexicans, no less than the vintners of northern California, felt constrained to borrow the appellations of Europe for their local wines.

Upstairs in our room after dinner I dressed for bed and settled in with a novel. Suddenly there was a tremendous explosion. Once in World War II I had walked out on the fantail of a troop transport just as her five-inch stern gun fired. As a result, I am a bit deaf in one ear to this day. This explosion seemed hardly less concussive. It was immediately followed by the whine of spinning metal, and finally a great clang. I had been right. The firecrackers sold in the store were powerful enough to blow the lid off a garbage can.

A few moments later, as if activated by this signal, the jukebox blasted on at the dancefloor across the road, pouring out a barrage of Mexican rock, a genre that combines the worst of American rock and Mexican folk music. It was turned up full volume. The sound bounced off the mountains and crashed against our windows. Intermittently it was punctuated by explosions of such force that our bed shook.

The bombardment continued without letup. It was impossible to sleep and hard enough to read. Then the lights went out and the jukebox fell silent. It was only ten o'clock. Mr. Villareal, evidently, had an ingenious way of imposing curfew. He simply turned his generator off. Without light and music, his festive customers would be obliged to pursue less noisy diversions in the soft Baja night. The firecrackers, alas, murdered sleep for another hour. Then merciful silence.

In the morning I raised the blind and looked out over the valley, pale yellow in the sun just rising over the dark mountains. It looked as lovely and peaceful as it must have looked when the padres had first come that way nearly two hundred years before.

Besides boning up on generators and butane in the past months, I had been searching the Baja shelves of the Los Angeles Public Library for the history of Baja, and especially this valley and its port, which I had come to think of as my own country. And I knew that it was right here, just across the road from Mr. Villareal's establishment, that the Baja missionary period had come to its inglorious end.

Early in the sixteenth century, when Hernando Cortez conquered Mexico for God and king, the peninsula was thought to be an island, and was thus named "California," after a fabled island in a popular romance of the day. After subjugating the Aztecs, Cortez himself crossed what we call the Gulf of California, or more romantically the Sea of Cortez, to start a colony at the present La Paz. It withered away in a year, nearly a century before the Pilgrims landed at Plymouth Rock.

Cortez had found pearls at La Paz, including the famed black pearls that were to ornament the crowns of Europe and lure pearl hunters to the bay for centuries. Repeatedly the viceroys of New Spain tried to colonize California, imagining it to be as paradisiacal as the island of the fable;

but all the expeditions and colonies were swallowed up or blown away.

A century and a half after Cortez gave up, the missionaries came. They stayed another 150 years; first the Jesuits, then the Franciscans, and, finally, the Dominicans. It was in the spring of 1791 that the Dominican padre Juan José Loriente founded the Misión Santo Tomás. His superior in this endeavor, I had discovered, was a padre named Gomez, a footnote that struck me as significant and reassuring.

Actually, Padre Loriente had first built his adobe mission a few miles down the river valley, on the road we take to reach Bocana. But he did not find the climate to his liking, and three years later he moved to the main valley, building again on the very site now occupied by Mr. Villareal's grotto, and from which the sounds of temporal revelry had reached us the night before.

At the height of the Dominican sojourn, the Spaniards oversaw the lives and nurtured the souls of several hundred Indians at Santo Tomás. They raised cattle and sheep and planted palms and olive groves and orchards of peach and pomegranate and fields of corn, beans, wheat, and barley. Their grapes were loaded on burros and carried over our own dirt road to Puerto Santo Tomás, where the harbor was deeper than at Ensenada, and put on ships for Portugal and Spain.

I felt the excitement of discovery as I saw from our window a stand of great old palms across the road, towering above the olive groves. Could these be the ones the Dominicans had planted?

We found Mr. Villareal tending his one gas pump, an ancient model pumped by hand. Yes, he assured us, the palm trees and part of the olive grove had been planted by the padres, and if we wished we could walk through the grove and see the ruins.

We crossed the road and walked through the beer garden and on through a gate into the olive grove. There were new trees, but among them were others whose trunks were so thick and gnarled as to leave no doubt of their antiquity. Beyond them, the palm trees stood eighty feet high above a pile of weathered adobe walls that still bore the traces of form and function. Their highest point was surmounted by a rude cross—two olive branches which had been wired together and stuck into the ruins, I suspected, by Mr. Villareal himself.

It was here, below these palms, that the last of the padres had finally yielded the whole peninsula to the Devil and walked away. In all, they had built a chain of thirty-two missions on this thorny peninsula. When the Spaniards came there had been perhaps seventy thousand Indians in Baja. They were naked and hungry; the most primitive people in America. Their only diversion from a mean existence occurred at the summer harvest of the pitahaya cactus, whose tasty red pulp and potent seeds dissolved all moral restraints. Then whole tribes flung themselves at each other, not in war, but in sexual frenzy, and family ties and taboos were momentarily forgotten.

The padres had hoped to elevate these aborigines through the plow and the catechism. Instead, they saw them exterminated by smallpox, syphilis, and other novelties that came with the sword and the cross. By the time the Dominicans abandoned Santo Tomás in 1849, the southern Baja tribes had quite vanished, and in the north there were hardly more than a thousand Indians left alive. Today, it is said, only a handful of their descendants remain, clinging to life in the mountains above Ensenada.

Ironically, the contemporary people of Baja are Roman Catholic, but like the Church itself, they are newcomers to the peninsula; immigrants who crossed the gulf from mainland Mexico to seek a new life in the land that history had forgotten.

CHAPTER FIVE

It was a warm, late summer morning as we set out from El Palomar for Bocana. The green had gone from the mountains and the fields of the *ejido* were dry and dusty. This was the Baja we were used to, and our reward would be all the sweeter when we reached the mouth of the river and tasted the air from the sea.

The road seemed better than I had remembered. I addressed the wheel with a reckless confidence as we lurched and skidded among the rocks and potholes. The road no longer cowed me. I knew, for one thing, that it had a pleasant ending, and I had driven it several times now without misfortune. Also, at the back of my mind was a bit of automotive lore from somewhere. The greater your speed over a rough road, the smoother the ride. Wasn't that the way it went? Of course there would be a point of diminishing return, but a good driver would anticipate it.

"Aren't you going too fast?" Denny shouted above the noise of the car.

"It doesn't pay to go too slow," I shouted back. I thought of explaining the principle, to set her mind at ease, but there was no use; the noise would drown out the finer points.

I heard her shout again and simultaneously saw the squirrel racing into my path. I jerked the wheel. The car yawed wildly. Then I saw the rock, large and sharp as an axe; too late. There was a wrenching thump. The wheel jumped in my hands. I wrestled the car back on course, but a moment later I heard the sickening *clump-a-flop-clump-a-flop* of a blown tire.

We came to a stop. Dead silence closed in.

"Anyway," she said, "you missed the squirrel."

I got out to inspect the damage. The front right tire was in shreds. The rim was mangled. There was no automobile club to be called by telephone. The only service station within twenty miles was the single gas pump of El Palomar. I would have to change the tire myself. It is a man's job, but one I have always despised and tried to avoid. Reluctantly, I opened the trunk and removed the spare, the jack, and the lug wrench. I pried the hub cap off and tried to loosen the lugs, but they seemed to be stuck fast. The tires were steel-belted, and I had never had one of them flat before.

"I can't do it," I said. "You'll have to hold the wrench on the nut, and I'll try pushing down on it with my leg."

She held the wrench on a nut. I planted a foot on the handle and shoved down, putting my whole leg into the thrust.

"Umph!" she said as the wrench slipped off the nut and she fell forward on her knuckles in the dust.

"You have to hold it fast," I said, "or my foot slips off."

"Why can't you hold the wrench," she suggested, "and use my leg to push it down?"

"Because my leg is stronger than yours," I explained.

At last, working together, we got the lugs off. I jacked up the car and horsed the wheel off and slipped the spare

on the bolts and lowered the car. It was hot in the road
and I was not accustomed to such exertions. I felt suddenly faint.

"I may be having a heart attack," I said. "I'll just cross
the road and rest in the shade of the trees. You think you
can tighten up those lug nuts?"

I sank against the trunk of an oak tree, breathing
heavily. I heard a squeal and laughter, and a woman and
three small children came running down the road, chasing
a runaway piglet. The woman saw me and laughed and ran
on. She would be of no help; she had her own pursuits.

I saw that Denny was trying to tighten the nuts by
pushing up on the wrench instead of down, thus losing the
assistance of gravity.

"Don't push up," I called out to her, "push down."

"They're as tight as I can get them."

"Well, then, good. Just put the hub cap on and we'll
be off."

"How are you feeling?" she asked.

"A bit weak," I said, "but I think the worst of it is
over."

We found Gomez behind the counter in his store. I told
him the story of our misadventure.

"But you saved the life of the little squirrel?"

"We think so," Denny said.

"*Gracias a Dios,*" said Gomez. "That is good. Would
you like a nice cold beer?"

Mrs. Gomez prepared a lunch of fried rock cod and
abalone and afterward we sat at the table in the tiny
kitchen and I showed Gomez the plan I had drawn. It was
for a simple rectangular house, with two bedrooms, a

bath, and a living space and kitchen combined. I had kept it small and compact.

"Jack," said Gomez, "you are an artist. Your plan is beautiful."

His tone, though, didn't seem to fit the generous words. I sensed an underlying reserve.

"As you know," I said, "we're expecting to keep this under ten thousand."

"Of course."

"Well, then," I said, "I think we're ready to go ahead. What's the next step?"

"Tomorrow," said Gomez, "we go to Ensenada to record your lease, and then I will give your plan to my architect, in Tijuana, for the blueprints. There is nothing to worry about."

"How is our lot?" I asked him. "Has it moved again?"

"Your lot," said Gomez, "it is very happy."

We stayed that night in Gomez's new cabin, which was to accommodate us many nights until the house was far enough along for us to use it as a weekend shelter. The cabin was built on a knoll overlooking the store and the lagoon. It was of brick and tile, like the two American houses, with indoor plumbing. Gomez had built it as a rental unit, and it was a world apart from the nearby wooden shack in which he and Mrs. Gomez stayed. We wondered if Mrs. Gomez didn't sometimes covet the new cabin herself, and we wished they would move into it instead of renting it out; but evidently that was not in Gomez's economic scheme.

In the morning we drove early into Ensenada for breakfast and at ten o'clock met Gomez, as arranged, at the federal recorder's office. Gomez had the required copies of the lease on hand. It was, in fact, a contract of usufruct, under which Romulo Gomez Monroy (the Monroy being his mother's maiden name), owner of "a piece of rustic land located in the Channel of Santo Tomás, Jurisdiction of Santo Tomás, Municipality of Ensenada, State of Baja California, with an area of 891,621 square meters," granted to Jack Smith and Mary Denise Smith, the *usufructuarios,* the right to use a fraction of this land for ten years, after which the owner might issue a new contract of usufruct for another ten years.

I wasn't sure I understood the full meaning of the term usufruct and the prerogatives it might convey, and it appeared clear that the option of renewing the lease was Gomez's, not ours. Still, on that point we had his word.

The statement that Romulo Gomez was the owner of exactly 891,621 square meters of rustic land was of course his own statement, and carried with it no official stamp. Nonetheless, it was in writing; it sounded precise and concrete; it smacked of surveyor's instruments and entries in record books, and I found it comforting.

Getting the lease recorded turned out to be an expedition. Our presence was required before the clerks and notaries of three different bureaus, at various levels of government, and in various parts of town. Our next-to-last stop was at the National Bank of Mexico, where it was necessary to pay eighty dollars American in fees. This was a contingency we had innocently not foreseen, and, in fact, we did not at once grasp what was required of us. Gomez was too diffident to tell us. He is never the first to mention money directly. I sensed his embarrassment.

"What is it, Romulo?" I said. "Is something wrong?"

"It is all right," he said. "I will take care of it."

"Take care of what?"

"It is all right. Don't worry. It is only eighty dollars."

"Eighty dollars?"

We must buy eighty dollars' worth of stamps, he explained, which we would then take to yet another office as proof that we had paid our federal fees.

Denny and I made a hurried accounting of our cash. Between us we had less than thirty dollars. Credit cards were of no use.

"Don't worry," said Gomez. He reached for his wallet and withdrew a packet of American bills. They added up to exactly eighty dollars. Gomez had anticipated our predicament and come prepared.

"I'll write you a check," I told him.

"As you wish," he said.

In twenty minutes more it was official. We were *usufructuarios,* leaseholders of a fraction of rustic land in the Channel of Santo Tomás.

Afterward we walked to Hussong's to seal our contract with a toast. Hussong's hadn't changed, that I could see, since the days when we had been habitués, sipping the peerless margaritas mixed by Tony, the bartender, and listening to the mariachi. It was nothing but a weathered frame saloon with a false front, like those of the old American West. Over the swinging doors was the hand-painted legend:

HUSSONG'S

Established 1882

So it was already there in 1884 when an American company took over Ensenada on a charter from the Mexican dictator Porfirio Díaz and brought about an astonishing industrial and real estate development. Cotton and woolen mills sprang up; shoe, soap, and match factories; distilleries and wineries. Agriculture and animal husbandry flourished. Gold flowed in from nearby strikes, and Bahía de Todos Santos began to rival San Francisco, at least in the minds of its promoters.

But it was an inflated prosperity, like the simultaneous boom in Los Angeles, and in 1888 it broke. The mines ran out. Drought came. The great design fell through. Díaz withdrew the charter and turned the town over to a British syndicate, which settled in to exploit the American company's leavings. Thus began what some Ensenadans were to call the "British oppression." They arrived in pongee shorts and pith helmets and dinner jackets, and with plans and promises worthy of an imperial race. They squeezed Ensenada dry, and in 1915, with Mexico on the rack of revolution, they sailed home to the mother isles, leaving nothing tangible behind but a genteel golf course.

Hussong's, one of the numerous local enterprises of a pioneer German family, had survived the American and the British occupations, and sunk back with Ensenada into a quarter-century of lassitude. It became the headquarters for a hard-drinking breed of American yachtsmen and expatriates for whom Ensenada was a haven from Southern California with its nine-to-five rat race and strident boosterism.

We hadn't been in Hussong's for perhaps five years. Nothing had changed but the dates of the calendars. No paintbrush had desecrated the hallowed walls. Incredibly, the stuffed goose still stood on the backbar. The grotesque heads carved from coconuts were still there, and the same oil paintings, hideous as nightmares. Tony was still behind the bar. He was grayer and heavier, but he worked with the same grace and aplomb. He looked up at us and smiled quickly. He remembered. It might have been only yesterday.

We ordered tequila, neat, to seal our contract. The three of us raised our glasses.

"To our little house," I said.

"To the most beautiful mansion," said Gomez, "in Baja California."

CHAPTER SIX

Gomez's architect in Tijuana was very busy. It was three months before the blueprints came in the mail one day to our house in Los Angeles.

They were beautiful. The legends were of course in Spanish, so that bedroom had become *recámara*, kitchen *cocina*, and living room *estancia*. Even the bar had been drawn in and labeled *barra*. The Spanish words made the project seem all the more romantic. The dimensions all seemed larger than the ones I had indicated, but I thought perhaps this had something to do with the architect's use of meters, instead of feet and inches.

I was upset, though, by the six-arch porch drawn in on the front elevation. I had greatly admired the porch of the Millard house, but I had told Gomez we could not afford a porch; it was a needless extra. Still, in the blueprints before me now the porch looked so handsome, and so Mexican, I knew immediately that Gomez had prevailed again. Now that I had seen this rendering, I would never be able to give it up.

With the blueprints came a sheet of specifications listing every item of the proposed construction, and its estimated cost. We noted that the blueprints themselves, along with their registration and approval by the health department, the state building department, and the city building department, had come to $180. That seemed reasonable enough, and I was glad to know they had been scanned by so many authoritative eyes.

The itemized list looked businesslike and thorough. At first glance, the estimated costs seemed unexceptionable. Grading and excavation, $410; fireplace, $300; windows, $240; sewer and septic tank, $340; kitchen shelves, $180; porch with six arches, $800.

That last one ought to have been a jolt, but I wasn't shaken. In my mind was that vision in the blueprints. My opposition had dissolved. But the next item puzzled and alarmed me.

" 'Bathroom cabinet and beach pebble top, $326,' " I read. "What's that?"

"That was your idea," Denny said. "You don't remember?"

It came back. That first day, Gomez had shown us the interior of the Millard house, its owners being away. The Millard house had been part of the enchantment, with its high, beamed ceilings, its dazzling tile and graceful arched doorways and niches. And I had especially admired the top of the bathroom cabinet, which was not of the usual tile or synthetic, but of smooth round pebbles, richly and multifariously colored, imbedded in some translucent mastic. The pebbles had come from the pebble beach below our lot, the same lode that was to supply the pebble business Thomson had told me about that day in the cafeteria.

"You insisted we had to have one exactly like it, because it was so ingenious. I think that was the word."

"Indigenous," I said.

I was obliged to swallow the pebbles, but the next item

wouldn't go down at all. "What's this? Main door, carved —a hundred and ninety dollars?"

"I don't remember anything said at all about the door."

"Good Lord," I said. "A hundred and ninety dollars for a *door?*"

I was not shocked or even surprised, though, by the sum at the bottom of the list. Gomez had brought it in for under thirteen thousand dollars. It was three thousand dollars more than the outside figure I had given him, of course, but deep down I was not displeased. We were going to have a sturdy Mexican house, not a plaster eggshell, and I had no doubt it would have cost three times as much in Los Angeles. All the same, Gomez had once more shown an exasperating disregard for my instructions, and I would have to speak firmly to him. He must realize that we could not embrace his every chauvinistic fancy and digression. And I was certainly going to have it out with him about the $190 door.

I was troubled by an inventory of appliances that were to be supplied "by owner." Bathroom lavatory, gas range, refrigerator, water heater, toilet, wrought iron lamps, and kitchen sink. At the least, I guessed, these would add up to a sizeable amount. Worse, we would have to buy them in Los Angeles and either pay a prohibitive duty or try to smuggle them across the border, and I had no wish to affront the Mexican government and take the risk of ending my days in a Mexican prison. Mexican prisons, I had heard, were no pleasanter than prisons in any other country.

Finally the terms were set forth as $4,500 down, $4,000 when the walls were up, and the balance on completion of the house. The document was signed "Romulo

Gomez Monroy, Bocana de Santo Tomás, Baja Cfa., Mexico."

What I had in my hands, I realized, was a hard contract for a fantasy. I wanted to telephone Gomez at once, but it was a day on which he would be at Bocana, beyond our reach. I would have to wait until Tuesday night when he returned to Tijuana.

Denny meanwhile had lost interest in the itemized costs and was examining a little sheet of paper on which had been typed, evidently by the architect, a list of questions for the owner.

"*'Que color de pintura en el techo?'*" she read aloud. "*'Que color de azulejo? Que color en las puertas? Que medida mosaico? Si quieren vaciado en la puerta de la cocina? . . .'* Oh, this is going to be fun."

Instead of phoning Gomez, we decided to wait and drive down on the weekend. It was never very satisfactory talking to Gomez over the telephone. To understand him fully it was sometimes necessary to look into his eyes.

It was winter, but that is a good time of year at Bahía Santo Tomás. The hills are brown from the summer, but the sky is clear blue and the wind is warm; the summer people in their campers are gone and the feeling of isolation is deep and purifying.

Gomez was in his store. He took us into the kitchen, where Mrs. Gomez was chopping onions for her salsa and Marisa was making tortillas, turning and patting them in her hands in the same way Cortez had found Mexican women making tortillas 450 years before her.

We had a drink of tequila and I broached the subject of the contract. I reminded him that the estimate was three thousand dollars over the figure I had specified as our limit, not to mention the appliances that were to be supplied "by owner."

"Of course, the house is going to cost a little more than I estimated," said Gomez, "because it is much larger now."

"Larger? Larger than what?"

"It is larger than your plans."

"How did that happen?"

"It is the fault of the bathroom."

"I don't understand."

Gomez explained. I had told him I wanted a pebble top exactly like the Millards'. The Millards' pebble top was seven feet long. To get a seven-foot top into the bathroom, the architect in Tijuana had been obliged to make the bathroom bigger.

"And of course," said Gomez, "to make the bathroom bigger he had to make the whole house bigger."

"I see," I said. It had evidently not occurred to him to make the cabinet smaller; or perhaps it had, and he had rejected the idea.

"You will have a mansion," he said.

"Well, all right," I said. "That was my fault. But what's this about the main door—a hundred and ninety dollars? Are you sure you don't mean nineteen dollars?"

"The door comes from Guadalajara," he said. "No place else in the world do they make such beautiful doors."

"And it actually costs a hundred and ninety dollars?"

"*Sí.* It is a bargain."

I made it plain that we would do without a carved door from Guadalajara, even if it was the most beautiful door in the world, and that Gomez could get one from Sears for $19, or maybe $29.

Gomez smiled as if we were sharing a joke. It was obvious that no door from Sears would ever bar our threshold.

"Okay, Jack," he said. "You don't want a Guadalajara door? I will make your door myself."

"Good," I said. "That's fine." I also told him it would be out of the question for us to supply the lavatory, stove, refrigerator, water heater, toilet, wrought iron lamps, and kitchen sink as he had specified.

"We would appreciate it if you could round them up for us in Mexico," I said. "Of course we would expect to pay."

"If you wish."

I told Gomez he would hear from us in a week or so; as soon as I could get the money out of savings for the down payment.

"We're not sure, though," I told him, "how soon we can have the balance. I wouldn't want the work to get ahead of us."

He laid a hand lightly on my shoulder. "Jack," he said, "I wish you owed me a million dollars."

"Anyway," I told Denny later as we walked up to the cabin, "I knocked out the Guadalajara door."

"Yes," she said, "you handled him very well."

The next morning we drove over the hill to our site on the plateau and looked out at our view through the car window, trying to imagine what it would soon be like looking out of the window of our own house.

We left the car and climbed down a lava seawall to the tidepools. They shone like coins in a Camelot of dark rock castles. The tidepools seemed pristine. They had escaped man's urge to plunder and lay waste. Here there was no need to search for life; among the tidepools it is hard enough not to walk on it. Every square inch is contested. Struggle is constant, and so is renewal.

Everything that is not rock is living. Even the rock is not to be trusted. If it squishes underfoot it may be algae or a rockweed, covering and shielding tiny marine animals from too much sea and sun. Or one may walk on what appears to be gray rock, only to find on a close inspection that it is a honeycombed colony of thousands of tube worms, each no bigger than a pinhead and encased in its tiny shell, which is thought to be made of sand. Every living thing is either feeding or reproducing; or from the opposite point of view, being eaten or being born. In color the rock is mauve to black, with that agonized look of rock thrown up from volcanoes when the earth was new, a memento of God's wrath, or perhaps His ecstasy.

I made my way out to a point where the rocks stand against the blows of the sea. Here they are purpled with mussels or carpeted gray beige with colonies of gooseneck barnacles. A bright orange starfish caught my eye, orange velvet with lines of little white dots like lace, and beside it a larger purple starfish, also in white lace, the two of them like ladies' evening bags tossed on a couch.

Rock crabs ran from my step, then turned belligerently to face me, claws upraised like the gloved hands of old-time prizefighters. I squatted to study a cluster of turban snails in a still pool. Their shells are like Oriental turbans of purple, black, and tan, the size of thimbles. I tried lifting one, but he held. Then one raised up on hairy legs and scrambled away. It was no snail, but a hermit crab, running off with his stolen house.

I had been reading *Between Pacific Tides,* by the late Ed Ricketts, the marine biologist who was the beloved Doc of

Steinbeck's *Cannery Row*. Doc's book is the bible of serious beachcombers, and it was gratifying to have read about some improbable creature such as the hermit crab, and then to find him in the tidepools, behaving just as Doc said he would. Hermit crabs are the Keystone Kops of the tidepools.

Suddenly I found myself impulsively interfering. I reached out with a hand and knocked the hermit crab over with a finger. A comic arm reached out and righted the shell. It was like watching the circus thin man get into a six-foot hat.

The bottom of the pool was a bed of sea anemones. They were open, waiting, as lovely as daisies with green petals and beige centers; as deadly as Medusa. "Voracious feeders," Doc called them, with tentacles to paralyze their prey and powerful juices to digest them.

I pulled at a turban snail. He held fast. I pulled and twisted and at last he came loose with a viscous snap. I dropped him into the yielding center of an anemone. The anemone began to undulate. The green petals waved and folded in over the turban and the anemone closed in on itself like a devouring mouth.

I felt a twinge of guilt. I had known power, and abused it. In the banal phrase of old Bette Davis movies, I had played God.

But nothing in nature is wasted. All is eventually redeemed. When the anemone in time digested the snail and ejected his pretty shell, some hermit crab would have a new house.

In the long view I must consider myself benign.

CHAPTER SEVEN

In the following week our resolution wavered, or at least mine did. I don't believe now that my wife ever faltered or looked back, from the day we first stood on the land and made our silent pact.

But when it came down to tapping our savings and turning over to Gomez what to us was a large sum of money, I was immobilized by misgivings. I have a prudent side, as well as a romantic, and it was demanding to be heard.

"You're out of your mind," it insisted. And forthwith it stated its case, a very strong case indeed. We stood on a precipice, and were about to jump. We were about to commit a large part of our savings, and eventually much more, how much more no one could say, to a man we hardly knew, a man who was not bonded and not subject to American law, for the construction of a house in a foreign country on an unmarked lot we did not own and could never own. We were counting on the dubious guarantees of a short-term lease whose renewal was at the pleasure of the landowner. And if the house were built, whose house would it be? Could we *own* a house on land we didn't own? Weren't we building, in effect, a house for Gomez? What were the legal documents of record? Nothing we knew of but a ten-year lease.

What if the water supply ran dry? Where was the guarantee of water? Who guaranteed to keep the dirt road open? They hadn't even repaired the broken cattleguard. What if the border were closed some day? What if the revolution came?

Even if everything else turned out all right, how often could we enjoy a house that was five or six hours away, a whole day's driving out of a two-day weekend?

Consider the hidden costs and wear and tear. How many flat tires would we have, and ruptured shock absorbers? And the personal hazards. The tidepools and castles at the foot of the cliffs were beautiful, and one careless step could send you plunging to your death. You would be more truly isolated, remember, than if you had built in the High Sierra, where phones and helicopters and rangers were close at hand. If you broke a leg or a rattlesnake bit you (and the rattler is ubiquitous in Baja) it would take you an hour and a half to reach a doctor, a doctor who might know as little English as you knew Spanish.

What if disenchantment set in? Could you sell the house? What would you offer as proof of ownership? Who would buy a house he couldn't own, from a man who didn't own it? Who except you?

You say you've already paid up your lease, and unless you build you've wasted all that money? Remember the first rule of poker—don't send good money after bad. Get out. Build your hideaway closer to home, on American soil, with all the safeguards of American law. Better yet, invest in a condominium. You can't go wrong in California real estate. In ten years you can double your money, instead of watching it expire with a foreign lease.

It was a formidable assault. I was demoralized. My prudent side was right.

"Did you withdraw the money yet," Denny asked one evening that week, "for Gomez?"

"No," I said. "I've been doing some thinking."

She was doing her ironing in the living room, a practice adopted to permit the amelioration of this dreary task by the simultaneous watching of television. Her iron stopped. She looked up. Her face clouded. She waited.

"I think we're making a mistake," I said. "Maybe we ought to get out before we're in too deep."

"Why?"

I gave her all the questions and arguments of prudence. Most of them, it seemed to me, would carry weight with a woman. After all, traditionally they were homemakers and conservators, weren't they? They were not easily drawn far from the home fires or persuaded to rob the nest egg in the pursuit of folly.

"I thought we agreed," she said in a voice that was tremulous with disappointment, "that we wanted some adventure."

Yes, I did remember. That first night, driving back to Los Angeles from Bocana, exhilarated by our meeting with Gomez and our unspoken decision out there on the bluffs, we had agreed we would always look upon our undertaking as an adventure; and whatever happened, no matter how bad it might turn out, we would never blame each other.

Adventure was exactly what we needed in our lives. I had even remembered the little poem by Robert Frost—

> The people
> I want to hear
> About are the
> People who
> Take risks.

Our children were grown, our home was paid for, our economic future was as secure as Social Security and retirement plans could make it. Perhaps that was exactly where the trouble lay. We had walled ourselves in, as safe as people could be against the unpredictable. But we felt restless and unused. Were comfort and security the ultimate goals of the species? Gomez had shown us a way out. He offered challenge and perils and a chance to spend our energies and test our courage. He offered us a mansion whose dimensions could not be expressed in either feet or meters.

"Don't worry," I said, "I'll get the money out tomorrow."

I tried to appear nonchalant as I handed the teller my withdrawal slip the next morning, but I felt lightheaded, and there was a tautness in my stomach. This was the point of no return. I took the check for $4,500 and slipped it into my wallet. It was the largest sum of my *own* money I had ever held in my hand.

We decided not to go to Bocana to deliver the check. I was afraid the handing over of so gross a sum would embarrass Gomez. It was easier to put it in an envelope and send it to his address in Tijuana, together with a short note advising him to commence with the project; to give him, as he called it, "the green light."

A week went by without a word from Gomez; then another. He might have telephoned to say he had received the money, or at least sent us a note. I began to worry. Perhaps the money had never reached him. Who knew what might happen to a letter in the international mails? I decided to phone him.

"*Bueno*," said Gomez.

"*Buenos días,*" I said. "This is Jack."

"*Cómo está usted?*"

"*Muy bien.*"

"And your wife? She is well?"

"She's fine. And Delia—she is all right?"

"Of course. She is fine."

"Romulo, we wondered whether you got the check?"

"The check? Oh, yes. *Sí, señor. Muchas gracias.*"

"Fine. Fine. We just wanted to make sure. When do you think you can start the house?"

"Very soon, *señor.* Don't worry. But first I must buy the lumber and the bricks. And my crew, they have gone to Ensenada. It will take some time."

At this point, I was in no hurry. The down payment had depleted our ready reserve, and I wanted to build it up again before the walls were up and the second payment fell due.

It was another month, though, before Gomez could get his equipment and materials on the building site and round up his scattered crew. At last he telephoned to tell us the work had begun.

"Wonderful!" I exclaimed. "We don't want to rush you, Romulo, but how long do you think it will take?"

"In four months, Jack, your house will be finished."

The news was exciting. We hurried down to Bocana to witness this historic beginning, simply to absorb the reality of it. In the months to come, when we were running on our treadmill to keep abreast of the costs, we would be sustained by our memory of the broken ground.

We drove down on a Saturday morning and stopped at the store, but Gomez wasn't in.

"He's over on your job," said Mrs. Gomez. *Your job.* I liked the sound of it.

"The men work on Saturday?"

"Oh, yes, the men work every day but Sunday."

We pushed on, too excited to tarry with Mrs. Gomez for a cup of coffee. We passed the Millard house and the Luczynski house, and then we saw Gomez and his men standing in the road, directly in our path. They were surrounded by a rectangle of new foundation trenches. I stopped the car and stared. It was a moment before the significance of this phenomenon fully penetrated.

"My God!" I said. "He's building our house in the middle of the road!"

"Yes. It looks as if our lot has moved again."

It was true. If these trenches marked the outlines of our house, and no other explanation seemed likely, then our lot had moved a hundred feet up the hill, away from the sea, and our house would stand astride what had been the only artery of traffic between Bocana and the port. A detour had been cut, I saw, to bypass the building site. The arrogance of it was astounding.

"*Buenos días,*" shouted Gomez, walking toward the car. "*Cómo están ustedes?*"

"*Buenos días,*" I said as we got out of the car. "You are building the house in the road?"

"Oh, yes," said Gomez.

"But why?"

"Because the road," said Gomez, "it has the most beautiful view."

We stayed in the cabin that night and the next morning we set out on a hike to a place where, according to Gomez, a herd of sea lions lived. It was our hope that in the months to come, while the house was building, we could explore and experience our landscape, and deepen our feeling for it. Thus, when at last we moved into the house we would not be strangers.

It was a rigorous hike for city people used to automobiles and elevators. The path rose and fell over the backs of three or four rocky points that thrust out into the sea, creating dramatic coves, and sometimes it was driven inland by the ruggedness of the shore.

Finally we came to the place he had told us about; a great tumble of rocks; a primeval disaster; sculptured grottoes of eroded stone, tamed and polished, and mansions of purple lava, frozen in eternal fury.

We heard a sea lion bark, a sound much like the bark of our Airedale, and saw a huge old bull, mahogany red, on the crest of an island rock, his head thrown back as he trumpeted a warning to his dozing harem. Other heads appeared, necks arched, eyes rolling. Several cows unstuck themselves from the rock and waddled to its edge, looking tentatively down into the swirling sea, as if they'd really rather not, then one by one they flipped in. Their master's voice had spoken.

I climbed down into the grotto among the tidepools. They were larger and deeper than any I had ever seen, almost large and deep enough to dive into, and bright as diamonds, their walls carpeted with green anemones and purple urchins. I saw an orange starfish pasted to a rock, and then another flat out in a shallow pool, and then I counted them—a dozen starfish—orange, beige, and mauve velvet under white lace mantillas—all within my sight at once.

A great, long-necked bird stood on a pinnacle, watching. I looked all about. There was nothing anywhere to show that any human being had ever stood here before us.

Not a beer can, not a gum wrapper, not a bottle cap, not a piece of Kleenex. There was no sound but the wash of the ebb tide among the rocks, an occasional protest from the sea lions, the wind, and the cry of gulls.

Suddenly I was there, alone—ten thousand years B.C., at the dawn.

"Where *are* you?" It was my mate, calling me back.

"Right here," I shouted, my voice flying off on the wind. "Don't worry. I'm *all right.*"

I didn't want her to know how far away I had been.

The next morning we walked over to the building site and found two of Gomez's men unloading a truck full of large stones, some of them big as basketballs. They were dropping the stones into the bottom of the foundation trenches.

"Very clever," I told Denny. "You see what he's doing? He's going to save himself some concrete."

I noticed that a shallow ditch struck off through the bush toward the hill above the Millard and Luczynski houses. The reservoir Gomez had spoken of must be up there somewhere, and the ditch was for our water pipe. So there really was a reservoir. I was annoyed with myself for ever having doubted it.

Suddenly Denny said, "Here he comes."

The pickup was grinding over the hill in a ball of sunlit dust. One of Gomez's dogs loped out ahead of it in the road. Another was maneuvering up the hill among the sage and cactus.

"I only see two dogs," I said. We had never seen Gomez in the field without all four. They were his entourage.

"I think I see them in the back of the truck."

The truck disappeared for half a minute behind a shoulder of the hill and reappeared on the old road, the part of it Gomez had bypassed for our house. That was one of the advantages of building in the road—it gave you a private driveway.

"Buenos días," shouted Gomez as the truck pulled up beside us. Two dogs leaped out of the back and joined the others in an exploration of the landscape. After the greetings were over I asked Gomez how long he thought it would be before the foundation was finished.

"It takes time," he explained, "to gather up these beautiful stones. They are very heavy. But now your house will be built on rock. It will last five hundred years."

"Do you think you'll have it done next week?" I asked.

"First we must bring the water from the reservoir, to make the concrete."

"Wonderful!" Denny exclaimed. "If we have water, I can plant my oleanders."

"It looks like the ditch is finished," I said.

"Sí, señor. The ditch is finished. But we must wait for the pipe."

"You have no pipe?"

"We must have plastic pipe. It will last five hundred years. But it is made in the United States, of course. It will take a little time."

"You're having trouble getting it across the border?"

He shrugged amiably. "We shall see. Everything must be arranged."

It was right at that point, I believe, that Denny and I adjusted to the tempo of Baja. Everything would take a little time; but then it would last five hundred years. Never again, I promised myself, would I subject Romulo Gomez to such an inquisition. We would be patient; let the house take its time, while we learned more about the land and the beaches and coves that had been waiting for our footsteps a million years.

"Romulo," I said, "I would like to see the reservoir."

"You want to see the reservoir? *Sí, señor.*"

We got into the pickup and he drove us back over the road to a fork that ran steeply up to the reservoir. It was a rectangular concrete basin, sunken like a swimming pool and covered by a low wooden house with a gable roof. Gomez opened a shutter through which we peered into the depths. Sunlight filtered through the wood walls of the shelter, giving an opal brightness to the water. Its surface appeared no more than a foot or two above the bottom.

"It looks very low," I said.

"The water is on its way right now," said Gomez.

Outside at the lower end an outlet valve was connected to a plastic pipe that set off down the hill and vanished under the sand and brush. A new ditch seemed to be heading off toward our lease. I walked around the reservoir but could see no intake line.

"How do you get the water into the well?" I asked.

"Here she comes."

A battered old water truck was crawling up the hill. It looked as if it had once been yellow, but its body had turned to rust. It had taken on the color of the Baja land, and looked as old. It labored up to the reservoir and the driver backed it expertly up to the open window.

A youth jumped out, tall and slim. It was Pepe, the Gomezes' younger son. He was a beautiful lad, with his father's physical grace. He had a drooping black mustache and long sideburns and his hair fell over his shoulders. He looked, indeed, like most any American youth of his generation.

Pepe stuck the tanker's outlet hose through the window and water began to gurgle into the reservoir. The tank was not very large, and I asked Pepe how many loads it would take to fill the reservoir.

"Twenty-four," he said unhappily.

The water might come from God, but it was taking a prodigious human effort to get it into the reservoir. In promising to provide us in perpetuity with this most vital of utilities, Gomez was certainly meeting *Dios* halfway.

In the morning we got up early to hike over to the port. We were early enough to see Pablo the fisherman putting out from Bocana through the surf in his old green skiff, shoving it into the breakers as fishermen before him had done for five thousand years. In a lull between waves he climbed quickly in and stood at his oars. We watched them reach and fall, reach and fall, like the legs of an insect crawling out to sea. Then the oars were folded in, Pablo yanked the little outboard into life, and the skiff headed for the kelp beds, where the bottom fish awaited Pablo's bait.

"If we're lucky," I said, "there'll be fresh fish for breakfast when we get back."

From Bocana to Puerto Santo Tomás, the port of Bahía Santo Tomás, it is three miles over a rutted road that climbs abruptly from the river mouth, gouges its way around a hill, here and there skirting awesome drops to the rocks, then undulates over a narrow desert plateau that breaks off high above the wonderfully variegated shore. Beyond Bocana, which has its lagoon and its wide crescent beach, there lies a necklace of beaches and coves, each with its own peculiar identity. One has a carpet of seashells, for reasons known only to the tides and cur-

rents; another is barren of shells but strewn with driftwood and flotsam; yet another, a crescent beach a quarter-
mile long, is buried under a deep shelf of pebbles; millions of them, richly colored and smooth as plums. This
is the treasure from which our bathroom cabinet top was
to come, and Thomson's and Gomez's fortune. Beyond
the pebble beach the cliffs turn yellow, great sculptured
walls of sandstone, and then the shore becomes impassable, a labyrinth of seaswept rocky spurs and promontories
that never dry.

Puerto Santo Tomás hardly seemed to deserve the
name port. We found a scatter of weathered shacks and
trailers, a row of scabrous cabins for rent, and a store that
was larger than Gomez's, but something short of a cor-
nucopia. Its staples evidently were beer, beans, and
fishing tackle.

But the point itself, marked on maps as Punta Santo
Tomás, was of a savage beauty that even its shabby encrus-
tations could not hide. It was a great black lava bulwark
against the ocean, offering itself to the heavy seas and
sheltering the bay.

There was a sheer drop to a hook of the bay where a
few aged fishing boats lay at their moorings like old dogs.
Two or three others were out on the bay in the kelp or
working the deeper coves for abalone. The men of the
port were out early, like Pablo, and it seemed deserted.
The women, if any, were out of sight. Only the dogs
waited for the boats to return.

The port had seen grander days. In my reading at the
public library I had learned that Juan Rodríguez Cabrillo,
the first European to see the peninsula's Pacific coast, had
put in here with his tiny caravels on September 14, 1542.
The intrepid Portuguese, sailing under the flag of Spain,

was searching for the Straits of Anian, a mythical passage from the Pacific to the Atlantic.

His log noted that he anchored off this point and sent a party ashore in a boat to look for food, firewood, and Indians. They returned to the flagship empty-handed, and Cabrillo sailed on to discover the bay of Ensenada. Like all good Roman Catholic navigators, Cabrillo had no trouble naming his find. He simply looked up the date in his calendar of saints' days and named it Santo Mateo, for St. Matthew, then sailed on to his death on an island off what is now the American city of Santa Barbara.

It was sixty years before another European came this way. Then, in November of 1602, nearly two decades before the Pilgrims sighted Cape Cod from the Mayflower, Sebastián Vizcaíno passed our point, hugging the shore as he sailed up the coast and into a strong northwestern, determined to circumnavigate the supposed island of California. A day or two later he, too, sailed into the bay of Ensenada, evidently finding it so beautiful he thought it deserving of more than one patron, so he changed its name from San Mateo to Bahía de Todos Santos—Bay of All the Saints—which it is called to this day.

For two centuries the Spanish galleons from Manila had sailed on our horizon, awkward, slow, and heavily laden with Oriental riches on their way to Acapulco. And doubtless this port had sheltered the British adventurers and the pirates that infested the peninsula, striking out to overhaul their clumsy prey, murder their scurvied crews, and make off with their precious cargoes.

Then came the great Chinese junks, incredibly, sailing straight across the Pacific from Cathay, fleets of them, to harvest the abalone that clung like sequins to the rocks of

Baja's bays. It was a traffic that lasted into the present century, and in which, I was to learn, our friend Gomez had at one time been a figure.

We climbed over the point and walked along a windy height until we came to a chimney that dropped to an exquisite little cove. I felt a thrill of discovery, as if we had come upon a secret place no man had ever seen. I thought of trying to reach it by descending the chimney, but there seemed to be no safe purchase on its walls. It would be foolish to risk a fall.

Then something flashed at the bottom of a tidepool; a shining like a mirror in the sun. For a moment I tried to imagine it was something else, but I knew well enough what it was. We were not, after all, the first. Someone had come before us, with a can of beer.

It was a long walk back over the road. When we reached Bocana we saw a black dot out in the bay. It grew gradually larger and then got up on its legs and crawled through the surf and onto the beach. Pablo was back. The bottom of his boat thrashed and glistened with red rock cod and striped sea bass, still putting up a fight. He dumped them into a tidepool and got out a knife and began carving out filets.

Mrs. Gomez had waited breakfast for us. Guacamole and chiles rellenos and, just in time, fried fish. Gomez opened a bottle of Misión Santo Tomas blanco, and as I raised my glass I was reminded that the Spaniards had indisputably brought one good thing, at least, to their fabled California.

CHAPTER EIGHT

For a few weeks we stayed away from Bocana. It was best to leave everything to Gomez. It all took time.

One weekend, though, our older son Curt drove down alone to see our land. He had just been discharged after four years in the Air Force, and was ready enough to spend a few days in a peaceful setting. When he came back we were eager to hear his report.

"The foundation is in," he said, "and there's a big pile of bricks on the site."

"How about the water?" his mother asked. "Is the pipe in?"

"Yes. The ditch isn't covered yet, so you can see the pipe. It must be connected and working or they couldn't have mixed the concrete."

"I have to get down there," she said.

"What's the hurry?" I said. "We've got nothing but a foundation."

"I want to plant my oleanders."

"I can't get away this weekend," I said. "It's impossible."

"Why can't I drive down alone?"

It was out of the question. She was a good enough driver, discounting a somewhat heavy foot. But the chances of a blowout or a breakdown were very high on that rough dirt road. It was unnerving to think of a woman alone at night out there with a flat or, worse, a ruptured gas tank or broken axle. And what if she had an accident in Tijuana or Ensenada? She might very well end up in jail. It was a consequence too dreadful to consider.

"I'll be perfectly all right," she said. "If I have trouble on the dirt road I'll just wait for help or sleep in the car or walk out."

"I don't like it. It's too risky."

"We agreed it was to be an adventure."

"If anything happened I'd feel responsible."

"I'm a liberated woman. Remember?"

She packed her car on Thursday night, loading a dozen oleander plants in the trunk, and left for Bocana on Friday after work. I had offered to let her take the Airedale for company and protection, but she wanted to go it alone.

"If I *did* have trouble," she said, *"I'd* have to take care of *him.*"

I knew she was right.

"Sure you can't go?" Her hands were already on the wheel and her voice had a tremor of excitement. She was enjoying this solo flight.

"No. I have too much to do."

"There's dog and cat food on the porch."

"Watch it on the dirt road. Don't go too fast."

"Don't forget to feed the cats."

"Don't forget to gas up in Ensenada, or you'll run out in the valley."

She waved and took off down the hill, a touch too fast, I thought.

It was the first of numerous weekends on which one or the other of us would have to make the trip alone. The city made heavy demands on us both, and we weren't always able to escape it together. Our faith in Gomez had deep-

ened with every month. All the same, he could be an
elusive and changeable man, like a cumulus cloud on a
windy day, and we were compelled to watch him closely,
not out of suspicion, but bewitchment.

For one thing, our visions and those of Gomez seemed
opposed beyond reconciliation. We thought of ourselves
as people of modest means, building a hideaway house on
the beach. In Gomez's eyes, we were rich Americans, for
whom money was no object, and he was building us a
mansion. It was my hope and conviction that somehow in
the end we would arrive simultaneously at the common
goal.

It was almost midnight Sunday when I heard her car pull
up. She was exhausted but happy, and quite pleased with
herself.

"How was the trip?"

"It was wonderful."

"You didn't have any trouble?"

"You might think so. I'm not sure."

She had blown a tire on the way home; not on the dirt
road, but right after she had left it, on the paved road in
the mountains above the valley. She had stood there in her
headlights, appraising her predicament, when a big white
car, a Cadillac, she thought, or maybe an Oldsmobile,
passed her going fast, squealed to a stop, and backed up.
A man in a gold silk suit got out and asked in English if
he could be of any assistance.

"A gold silk suit?"

"He was absolutely resplendent. A beautiful man."

He obviously had been dressed for some formal occasion, she said, and a beautiful woman in what appeared to
be a white evening dress waited silently in their car while

he changed my wife's wheel, being exquisitely careful not to soil his cuffs.

Then he had said *"Buenas noches, señora,"* with a little bow, and walked back to his car, rubbing his hands on a white handkerchief.

Now, I knew, she would never believe that anything bad could happen to her on that road. She had been enchanted forever by a Don Quixote in gold armor.

"Well, what's the news from Gomez?"

"Gomez is gone."

"Gone?" *Gomez gone?* All my misgivings, so long since relegated to the unconscious, welled up in a dark mushrooming cloud. "Gone *where?*"

"He's gone to Mexico City to see the president."

It was too much to absorb. Why in God's name would Gomez want to see the president of Mexico? Why would the president deign to see a man named Gomez, who owned a few acres of land two thousand miles away? Or *did* he own it? Was that what he wanted to see the president about? Was there now some cloud over his title?

"Who told you where he was?"

"Pepe."

"How long is he going to be gone?"

"Quien sabe?"

Who knows?

It was a Spanish phrase for which we were to find much use.

A few days after learning that Gomez had gone to Mexico City I phoned Tijuana, hoping I would find him safely home.

"Bueno." It was Mrs. Gomez.

"*Buenos días,* Delia," I said. "Romulo is not back from Mexico City?"

"No, Jack, he is not back."

"What's he doing in Mexico City, anyway?"

"It's business. That's all I know."

I had always suspected there was little about Gomez that Delia Gomez didn't know. In the kitchen down at Bocana I had too often seen her eyes smile at some supposedly man-to-man remark of his or mine. She was sometimes very amused by her husband, I thought, and very careful not to let it show too plainly, at least not in public. In some ways she was very much like my wife.

"Well, when will he be back?"

"Oh, maybe a week. Maybe two. Or three."

Another week passed and Gomez didn't return. Then one morning we received a card postmarked Taxco, which we found in our atlas only 50 miles or so from Mexico City. The message was as cryptic as its author:

> Dear Jack:
>   I hope when you take this in your hands, everything is perfect with you.
>   My best regards to you and your charming wife.
>   Tu amigo,
>   R. GOMEZ

"At least," I said, "we know he's alive. Or was."

I got away in the middle of the following week and drove down to Bocana alone. I wanted to see what was happening to the project, if anything, and to find out what I could about the itinerant Gomez.

It would not have surprised me to find that not a stone had been turned. But when I topped the rise and our plateau came into view, I saw the beginning of a wall on our land, half a mile away. All the old excitement returned. Gomez was not here, but his work was going on, as if his will and energy could be delivered by remote control.

Two men were at work, setting the large Mexican bricks into walls that were up to their knees. They looked up and smiled and shouted *"Buenos días,"* but we could communicate no further. I was annoyed with myself that I knew so little Spanish. The concrete floor had been poured but not finished, as in time it would be covered by red tile. But the rooms were laid out, and I walked among them, trying to imagine their ultimate dimensions and peering out through imaginary windows at the bay. Gomez had been right after all, about the view.

He had gouged out a level plot for the house to stand on, leaving a six-foot bank in the rising earth. My wife had planted the oleanders along the top of this bank, so they would screen us from the new road someday, and give us some color from our kitchen window. They looked wilted, and I thought I'd better give them some water.

The plastic pipeline down from the reservoir ended in a faucet to which a hose was attached. I picked up the end of the hose and turned the faucet on. No water came. Not even a gurgle. There was no pressure in the line. The men were watching me.

"No agua?" I said. *"Por las flores?"* It was an extraordinary effort; a whole sentence, almost, conjured up from high school Spanish. I soon realized it had been a mistake. There is no use speaking Spanish unless you have the

capacity for going on with it. Otherwise you simply give
a false impression of felicity in the language, and set off
a response that is rapid and utterly incomprehensible.

Both of the workmen loosed cascades of amiable
Spanish, none of which I understood explicitly, but whose
burden was obviously that, "Yes, there is no water." They
pointed up the hill toward the reservoir and held their
palms out empty.

"*Gracias,*" I said. "Don't worry. I'll look into it."

I drove up the hill to the reservoir, wondering if this
was to be a common occurrence. I parked and looked
through the open window down into the tank. It was dry;
nothing but a fine silt, the color of pearl, shining at the
bottom.

Pepe was in the store, sitting up on the back shelf with
his feet braced against the counter. Mexican music was
pouring from a transistor. He was alone. Since his father
had gone to Mexico City, his mother did not come down
to Bocana.

"The reservoir is empty," I said.

He nodded. "I know. I'm filling up the truck right
now."

I could hear the distant gasping of the one-cylinder
pump, but I couldn't remember having seen the tank truck
when I drove up. It should have been out back of the store
beside the well, shouldn't it?

"The well is broken," said Pepe. "I have to get the
water from the lagoon."

"From the lagoon?"

The lagoon lies between Gomez's store and the beach,
and is filled, I am told, with fresh water from the underground river in the canyon. Cattails grow all around its
edges, and the water is usually clear enough to swim in.

But now it was murky, and a family of mudhens had taken it over.

"I didn't know there were so many birds in it," I said.

"Wait till the ducks come," said Pepe. "Hundreds of ducks. They come up from the south, every year."

The old water truck was backed up to the edge of the lagoon, drinking up water through its thick black hose. The pump had been lugged down from the well and set in the mud at the edge of the water.

I had always wondered if Gomez's well might be the lagoon itself. Even if he got it from the well, the well was so close to the lagoon as to suggest that well and lagoon were the same. Of course we had never planned to drink the water. We would bring our drinking water down from Los Angeles in plastic jugs. But we had expected to wash our dishes in it and bathe in it. Oh, well. If mudhens and ducks could live in it, so could we. But there was no need to tell my wife.

We walked back to the store and Pepe opened us each a bottle of *cerveza*. The kitchen showed the absence of Mrs. Gomez's tidy touch. There was an open can on the table, a little pile of dishes in the sink, a greasy pan on the stove.

"It looks like you're batching," I said.

He shook his head. "Yeah. It's no good."

I wondered how young men like Pepe and Sergio liked their vigils down here at Bocana, now that they were grown and undoubtedly had a taste for the girls and the excitements of Tijuana.

"Maybe you should take a wife, Pepe," I suggested.

He smiled slyly. *"Quien sabe?"* he said. "Maybe I will."

"Pepe," I said abruptly, "why has your father gone to Mexico City?"

He shrugged. "It is something about the land."

My heart sank. "There is some question about the land? About the title?"

"Oh, no," Pepe said. There was no question about the title. His father owned the land. It was a matter of record. But now that the election was over, with the predictable result, there was a new president, and of course it was necessary for his father to see the appropriate people in the new government, including the president himself, if that should be the will of God, so that everything would remain the way it was.

I nodded. It was something like that in the United States. I could only wish Gomez success in his mission, whatever it was. *Vaya con Dios,* I thought. But I wondered what he had been doing in Taxco.

Gomez was gone a month. When he did at last come back my wife saw him before I did. She had gone down to Bocana one weekend in August when business held me in the city. These weekends of separation had become common, as I often found it hard to get away and she felt it necessary to look in on her oleanders. That was only an excuse, I knew. In truth her feeling for the house in Baja had deepened with every row of bricks. Long before the walls were finished she had begun referring to it as "my little *casa,*" a mixed idiom that seemed to express it well enough.

She was unintimidated by the perils of the road, although at this point she had already blown two tires and ruptured her gas tank on a rock. She seemed exhilarated rather than discouraged by such misadventures. She was discovering within herself a kind of courage that had not previously been called on, and was delighted at making its acquaintance.

Our friends thought we were both mad, and did not hesitate to say so. The men thought I was irresponsible in allowing her to drive into Mexico alone. They recounted the usual horror stories: Americans waylaid and robbed on the road; Americans dispossessed by an arbitrary law and a venal judiciary; Americans arrested for minor traffic accidents and thrown into foul jails.

To these well-meant reproaches I could only answer that it was perhaps more dangerous, statistically, to drive down to the supermarket in Los Angeles for a six-pack of beer than to drive our unpaved road in Baja.

"And, anyway," I would say, holding my hands palms up as Gomez so often did when confronted with a logical argument, "what can I do? She is a liberated woman."

This particular weekend she had invited our neighbor Sara Dalton to go with her, and they set out in high spirits.

"It's going to be dark when you hit the dirt road," I said, "but your headlights will show up the rocks and holes better than daylight. Just go slow and don't panic."

"I have never panicked yet," she said.

I assumed she was referring to the time I swerved to miss the squirrel and hit the rock, blowing the tire. That hadn't been panic; it had been an act of humanitarianism.

I had found that for twenty-four hours I enjoyed being home alone. When there are two people in a house, no matter how compatible, in some subtle way one always accommodates to the other. You are aware of this, however, only when you are alone, and then gradually it occurs to you that you have abandoned certain restraints. After the first day there is a tendency to stalk through the house in the nude; to sing *Pagliacci* at the top of your voice; to stand in front of the mirror and argue with yourself, vehemently, with gestures. And finally you rush the cocktail hour a bit and let the Airedale in to talk to.

On Saturday night Fred Dalton came over for a drink. He had begun talking to himself, too; unfortunately, the Daltons had been without a dog since they lost old Bosco, and he had no one to talk to.

We and the Daltons have lived across a canyon from each other on Mt. Washington for twenty-five years. They have an old, red-frame, three-story house with the lines of a tramp freighter, and a swimming pool which, in the summer, is the center of our social, intellectual, and physical life.

Dalton is a professor at the University of Southern California. His field has something to do with communications, but he is more deeply committed to his avocations, which include birdwatching, good bourbon, and the contemplative life. In that, we are much alike.

He likes to sit beside his pool in an old canvas chair, watching the wildlife on the hill through his spyglass. Sometimes he watches *us,* and once he phoned to tell us there was a burglar in our yard. It turned out to be me, however, out in the back yard in my pajamas stalking a tomcat.

Dalton has a strong feeling for Baja which derives like mine, perhaps, from frustration. In his youth he set out to sail its length in a ketch, but the ketch foundered on the rocks not far south of our own Bahía Santo Tomás, and was lost. All he saved was his spyglass.

Dalton was fascinated by our adventure, and almost as eager as we were for the house to be completed. That was one reason he had encouraged Sara to make the trip, though deep down I suspected she would have been happier at home by her pool with her *New Yorker* and her cookbooks.

"Have you been reading the paper?" Dalton asked as I made his first drink, "about that land development scandal in Baja? It looks like they've been selling Americans nothing but blue sky."

"It doesn't affect us," I said. "We're not in that kind of a deal."

Other friends, too, had been alarmed by the story. They had read that certain promoters, American as well as Mexican, were accused of making fraudulent claims and promises in offering land to Americans on the Baja riviera between Tijuana and Ensenada. We had passed the development many times, disturbed by its resemblance to jerry-built suburbs in Southern California, with big roadside signs and colored pennants blowing in the breeze. Some Americans alleged they had been led to believe they were actually purchasing the land, and that the luxuries and utilities promised by the agents had failed to materialize. But they had sued in American courts, which were without jurisdiction, except over the advertising and operations of the developers on the American side of the border.

"It's a bad show," I conceded to Dalton, "but it's nothing to do with us. We're dealing directly with Gomez, not some corporation."

"What I was wondering, though," Dalton said, "is how you know that Gomez actually owns the land."

"I asked him."

"I see."

"Listen, Dalt," I said. "We've always stood on solid ground with Gomez. He's been honest from the beginning. He told us we could only lease the land, not buy it, and he could only give us a ten-year lease, not twenty or ninety-nine years, like those other jokers were promising, because that was the law."

"Okay. You've got a ten-year lease. What then? How

do you know you'll get another one?"

"We have his word."

"There's no way you could buy the land?"

"Look at it this way. I wouldn't *want* to own that land. Why should it belong to me? Why should it belong to any American? Why should it belong to anybody at all, for that matter? Why should it belong to the human species? Land belongs to the earth."

It was more of a speech than I had meant to make, and it had exposed some ideas that I hadn't known I held.

"That's more land reform," said Dalton, "than even the Mexicans want."

"All any of us has," I carried on, "is a short-term lease on life. Who owns anything in perpetuity?"

Dalton nodded, sipping at his bourbon and water and thinking. "If you can't own the land," he said at last, "why then you can't own the house either, can you?"

It was a question that had troubled me, too, and I didn't know quite how to deal with it. We called it our house, Gomez called it our house, and yet the question was a stickler.

"Of course not," I said, trying to brazen it out. "It would be pointless, anyway. What good would it do to own the house? It's going to be solid brick, on a concrete slab. Nobody's ever going to move that house. It's going to be there as long as the Mayan pyramids. By God, Dalton, we're creating an archeological monument down there. We're making history."

"What we're saying, then," said Dalton, not catching the spirit of my fancy, "is that, actually, your house will belong to Gomez."

"When you get right down to it," I said, "yes. That is, it will if he owns the land."

Dalton was like most Americans, I thought. He worried about the wrong things, cherished the wrong values. Title. Possession. Permanence. They were all illusions, myth words, imaginary absolutes, part of our dreams of immortality. All I asked was that the tide come in on time and the sun come up and that Gomez keep the reservoir full.

The women got home Sunday at dusk. I had just begun to worry. They climbed out of the dusty car like weary Brownies home from a campout, unloading brown paper sacks full of beach pebbles and seashells and babbling about their adventures.

"What happened?" I asked when they were in the house and settled down with a highball.

"We saw this *thing*," said Sara Dalton, "in the road."

"What thing? What was it?"

"It was in the headlights," Denny said, "and at first we didn't know what it was."

"She hit the brakes. She kept her head."

"The face was all spotted and—"

"My God, it was dreadful!"

"What was it?"

"Sara thought it was a bandit."

"Yes. I yelled *'bandido, bandido!'* From my high school Spanish."

"I thought it was a cowboy wearing chaps, you know, because of those big brown spots."

They fell silent, reliving their vision. I waited.

"It turned out to be a cow," Denny said. "They look different at night."

I asked for the news. No matter how long or short our

absence from Bocana, there was always news, whether it was merely that one of Gomez's dogs had whelped, or that something visible had happened to the house.

"Gomez is back," she said.

"Thank God. What did he have to say?"

"He said the house will be finished in three months."

CHAPTER NINE

It was deep in September before we could both get away, but I had discovered that autumn was the season I liked best at Bocana. The summer intruders with their campers and motorcycles had gone back to their treadmills; the beaches were ours; the weather was beautiful and capricious.

It was late afternoon on a Friday when we started out. The exhilaration set in immediately as we drove inbound over the Pasadena Freeway, against the heavy traffic streaming out of downtown, but then we merged into the Santa Ana, the sluggish outbound mainstream, crawling down through that forest of billboards and past Disneyland until at last we broke free of the city's magnetic pull.

It was dark when we crossed the border. Somewhere below Rosarito Beach the moon rose out of the Baja hills. It was hot burnt orange; a Mexican moon; not the moon the astronauts had walked on, pale and bleak as a flare-lit battlefield. The moon rose and fell as the road climbed and sank and twisted, appearing here and there and nowhere, a paper moon manipulated by a drunken stagehand. When we turned into our valley to take the dirt road to the sea the moon left us. It was waiting, shining on the sea and the lagoon, when we reached the store.

The store was closed, but a light was on. The screen door at the rear swung open and a man came out into the moonlight. He wore a straw hat with the brim curled up at the sides, a black sweater, khaki trousers, and boots. He walked toward the car with a slow familiar grace and tipped his hat.

"*Buenas noches,*" he said, the voice faintly musical.

"*Buenas noches,*" I said. "You are back."

"Oh, yes."

"Is everything all right?"

"Of course," he said, "everything is all right."

I wanted to ask him about the land, the trip to Mexico, the card from Taxco, the reservoir, the house. But it is not profitable to talk business with Gomez in the moonlight. It is hard enough in daylight to tell reality from illusion in his presence.

Seeing him in the flesh was enough. I was reassured. He was our indispensable man. He was our strength, our fire and our water. He was our very earth. He was not, of course, the sun, moon, and tide. For those, we still must look to God.

We drove over to the house early Saturday morning and found him already on the job. There was no roof, but otherwise our house was beginning to look like a house. Inside, the carpenter was cutting wood for the rafters, using a circular saw powered by a noisy generator.

The men who had built the walls, Sebastían and Abel, were now at work on the porch. To my surprise, I saw that the frame was in place for the arches, but instead of there being six arches, as rendered so handsomely in the blueprints, there were only two very broad arches spanning the same space the six would have spanned.

"Romulo," I said, "what has happened to the porch? We were going to have six arches."

He smiled. "You are going to have a porch," he said, "like the porches of Guadalajara."

"Guadalajara?"

"*Sí, señor*. I have come from Guadalajara, and the porches are like this. It has been many years. I had forgotten how to make a porch."

"You were in Guadalajara on your trip?"

"*Sí, señor*. It is in Jalisco, the state where I was born. In Guadalajara are the most beautiful porches in Mexico."

"Did you bring a door?"

"You don't remember, *señor*? I am going to make the door myself."

The interior walls were up, and it occurred to me that we might sleep in the house at night now and then, in our sleeping bags, just to get the feel of it. The walls would shelter us from the northwesterly winds, which sometimes blew with gale force, and we would have the stars for a roof.

Something caught my eye in the little hallway connecting the two bedrooms and the bath. The door to the hallway from the living room was a graceful arch, as Gomez had planned, but I had no recollection of an arch in the hall itself. Yet there it was, an arched recess set deep in the wall. It was perhaps six feet wide and nine feet high, and its purpose was as much a mystery to me as its existence.

"You are a man of books. I have built you a bookcase," said Gomez.

"How much is it going to cost?" I asked.

It would be fine, a built-in bookcase, but I had determined to restrain Gomez from expressing his artistic whims at my expense. I had agreed to the porch, which had now shrunk from six arches to two, but I meant to draw the line at any others. Even Michelangelo had to be restrained.

"Don't worry about the cost, Jack," said Gomez.

"I have to worry about it, Romulo. We're not rich Americans, you know."

"Ah, Jack," he said, patting me on the back as he admired our bookcase, "I wish you owed me a million dollars."

That morning we climbed down to the driftwood beach, which is a small cove that lies between our house and the Luczynski house. It is clogged with driftwood and other objects cast up by the sea. I suppose there is a reason for everything, so there must be a reason why the sea chooses this particular cove as a repository for flotsam and jetsam, while the beach to the south is strewn with shells and the one to the north is buried under pebbles, smooth as eggs. It's as if the sea were a tidy old spinster who keeps all her mementos, each in its proper drawer.

I wondered what she had collected since I looked the last time. It is not an easy place to reach, so what you find there has come by sea, not by land. I always hope to find something that has come all the way from Hong Kong or Canton like the Chinese junks of two centuries ago.

The only way to get safely down to the driftwood beach without risking a bad fall is to walk a quarter-mile below it, where there is an easier descent, and then come back over the rocks. The rocks are passable only when the tide is out. Then you can walk among them, making a jump now and then over a swirling tidepool. If you were to try this when the tide was rising, though, you might stay too long and find it hard to get back.

It is easy to discover objects of human manufacture in the banks of driftwood. Man's work is unmistakable, especially the work turned out by his machines. From the gutted automobile by the road to the nail in the dust, it has his stamp.

The first thing that caught my eye was a white plastic jug. It lay in a stack of driftwood up high against the cliff, as far as the sea could shove it. It appeared to be a gallon jug; intact, except for the missing cap. I picked it up and turned it around, reading the words formed in the plastic.

PLASTIKING
One Gallon Liquid
NO DEPOSIT NO RETURN

One could only guess where it had come from; tossed overboard from some fishing boat, most likely, not far from here. I dropped it back into the driftwood. It was buoyant and indestructible. Maybe if no one claimed it the sea would fetch it back one stormy night and deliver it to some other shore. Like the Flying Dutchman it would sail on forever.

I picked up another one. It was also whole and shipshape.

PLASTICAINER
One U.S. Gallon

Plastiking? Plasticainer? It was inevitable. A plastic language for a plastic culture.

I saw Denny heading toward me over the rocks. She had her collecting bag and was treading carefully, looking for treasures. I dropped the Plasticainer in the driftwood and walked over to see what she was up to.

"Look what I found," she said. She had something between thumb and forefinger. It was a structure of bones, bell-shaped, twice the size of a thimble. It was made of radiating ribs and struts, like a birdcage or lantern. It was charming; a tiny masterpiece.

"It was inside the shell of a sea urchin," she said.

"Yes," I said. "It's a perfect Aristotle's lantern."

I had read about Aristotle's lantern in *Between Pacific Tides*. It was the movable jaw of the sea urchin, an exquisite structure whose resemblance to an ancient lantern Aristotle himself had remarked; and thus its name.

Someday we would put this Aristotle's lantern on our mantle, along with other treasures from the beach. What you find in the driftwood depends on what you're looking for.

The following month, November, I took a week off and went down to Bocana again to watch the house grow. I didn't want to hurry Gomez and I didn't want to interfere. But I wanted a sense of taking part in this project which we had come to think of as the main venture of our middle years.

I went to a Thrifty Drug Store and made our first purchase of furniture for the Baja house—a pair of foldup cots with pads, a pair of foldup aluminum and plastic chairs, a camping stove, and a Coleman lantern. I packed them in my car and added my sleeping bag and some Redi-Logs and set out. I was going to move in, ready or not. Denny would follow later that week in her own car.

I was pleased, as the house came into view, that some visible progress had been made. The roof was on; that is, the wooden subroof was on, though the Spanish terra cotta tiles had not been laid. But there were stacks of them on the ground. Gomez had been busy.

Another improvement, if it could be called that, caught my eye. It was a shack that stood up on the bank above the house, just above Denny's gallant row of oleanders. It had been made of waste wood and tarpaper and looked dilapidated already. It might have been standing there for twenty years.

Gomez was inside our house with Salvador, the carpenter. "*Buenos días, señor,*" he said with enthusiasm. He was proud of his progress. "You see? Very soon you are going to have a roof."

I had always admired houses with exposed rafters and beams, and now I stood in my own. From the walls the dark wood rafters slanted upward to the apex fifteen feet above us, where a handsome timber spanned the entire living room.

"Beautiful, Romulo," I said. "You are a great architect."

"It is American lumber," he said. "From the States. It is very expensive."

"You mean it is more expensive than you estimated?"

"*Sí, señor.* Your prices in America, they go up."

I couldn't deny it. What Gomez was telling me now was that the house would cost more than he had figured. We had long since accepted that. The house would cost what it had to cost. We had even abandoned the payment schedule. Gomez never asked for money, but he had ways of letting us know he could use it. He must pay cash on delivery for his materials, especially when they came from the United States. And sometimes it was necessary to pay duty at the border. Of that we could not complain. We had no wish to be involved in international smuggling, if only of such prosaic goods as plastic pipe. Whenever it was practical, though, we wanted Mexican materials, and when it was finished, it would be filled with Mexican furniture and Mexican art, such as we could afford. We were determined to be worthy of Gomez and his land.

Gomez and I walked outside and I noticed the shack again.

"It is for the men," he explained, "to live in."

"To live in? You mean the house is going to take that long?"

"Winter is coming, Jack. It will be too cold to sleep on the ground."

"Of course," I agreed. But I didn't like the thought that the house would take all winter. At the start he had told us it would take three months. It had been nearly nine months already, and we were still standing in an empty shell.

"Romulo, how much longer will it be?"

"Your house will be finished, *señor*, in three months."

Three months? I doubted it. Each three months only led to another three months. I was reminded of the celebrated theory of Zeno, the Greek philosopher. Even the fleet Achilles could never catch a tortoise, Zeno argued, if the tortoise had a head start, for each time Achilles reached the point from which the tortoise had started, the tortoise would have moved on.

I stowed our cots in what was to be the master bedroom, with a picture window on the bay, and set the folding chairs out on the porch. The porch was finished, and the wisdom of Gomez was once more apparent. The two wide arches gave a sweeping view of the bay and beyond it the open sea, a view unimpeded except for the single column at the center. Six arches, I saw now, would have given us a row of pillars to look at, instead of the sea and the sky.

That afternoon I set out for a walk on the pebble beach. I wanted to do some thinking. We are always turning things over in our minds, and perhaps in that casual or unconscious way we come to most of our decisions. Rarely does anyone sit down deliberately to think things through, to reach for some elusive truth, to grasp some ultimate reality.

I try it now and then, though, and sometimes I feel close to a breakthrough. When I was very young I believed that someday I would stop a moment to rest, perhaps on a mountain trail, or a promontory above the sea, and suddenly it would come to me, the meaning of life, as perfect and lovely as a soap bubble. It happened, didn't it, to heroes in novels?

Perhaps I had come close once, back in the early 1960s. I had got loose from the ties and weights of everyday affairs and was out in the space of my own imagination, buoyant and free. I knew that somehow I had broken through the material wall and into the infinite, and that in a moment the answer to everything would spin into view and I could reach out and haul it in like a fly ball.

Nothing came of it. I'm not sure the Great Ideas come to us when we're looking for them. Most likely they come when we don't expect them, like hiccups and hives. But it is worth trying. Meditation calms the spirit. I am not drawn to any of the cults, old or new. Group encounters would either bore or scare me. I would much prefer a picnic. Neither do I consider myself a likely candidate for divine inspiration. I'm afraid my credentials are not in order. But I try to remain available.

There was a Volkswagen with California plates on the bluff above the pebble beach, and when I took the path down to the beach I saw a small green plastic tent up high on the beach against the cliff. A man was sitting guru fashion in front of the tent, stroking a guitar. I walked down to the surf, giving the man a wide berth, so we wouldn't collapse each other's bubbles.

After a quarter of a mile the pebble beach changes character. The pebbles vanish; the beach becomes smooth flat sand, but it is strewn with great sculptured lava boulders that have broken off and tumbled down from the cliffs. The tide was out, and the boulders were pitted with tidepools, some of them perfect oval bowls, like bathroom washbasins, each with its sea anemones, lavender and palest green, and its clutch of polished colored pebbles, magnificent and bright in the trapped sea water.

Each bowl seemed exquisite beyond contriving. I wondered if I could move a single pebble without destroying such perfection, utterly upsetting the arrangement. Arrangement? That was hardly the word. Each pool was a phenomenon beyond the art of human hand and eye.

What then could account for such beauty? It must be chance; nothing more. Random chance. I remembered having read only recently some scientist's theory that man and the universe were simply the results of cosmic chance.

I lay back in the arms of a great sculptured sandstone chair in the cliff, a natural golden throne, my head against an antimacassar of bright green sea moss. I turned my face to the sun and shut my eyes, listening to the lullaby of the surf.

I don't know how long I had lain there in the clasp of

that stately sea throne, like Triton napping, when it suddenly occurred to me that I knew God's name. It came to me all at once, whole and final. His name was Random Chance.

Glowing with this light, I stirred myself and began to walk back over the beach toward the house. As I drew near the green tent I saw that the stranger had moved down closer to the surf. His legs were crossed as before, in the Lotus position, and the guitar lay across them, but he was not playing. He was simply looking out to sea. He had a full mustache and gentle eyes behind metal-rimmed glasses.

"It's a nice day," he said, as I came near.

"Yes. It is. It really is."

I didn't tell him about my revelation. I wasn't sure it was the kind of revelation that would be true for anyone else. Besides, he was obviously a meditative man. He could find out God's name for himself.

When I got back to the house, though, I told Gomez. As I knew, he was not without fantasies and revelations of his own.

"What do you think of it?" I asked.

"Jack," he said, "when you sit in the Mexican sun, you have to wear a Mexican sombrero."

"Well, then, Romulo—what *is* God's name?"

"God's name, of course," said Gomez, "is *Dios.*"

That night I stayed in the house for the first time. The soft wash of the surf put me to sleep and the sun woke me. I was aware first of stained wood ceiling and sturdy rafters; then of brick walls. The bricks were large and of a color that was neither ocher nor sienna; it was one of the many colors of the Baja earth, a burnt red-orange, for which I knew no name. The bricks were laid in thick layers of mortar, uneven enough to give witness that a human hand had been at work, not a machine. It was a work of art, that wall, and I made a vow that it would never be plastered over.

I had arranged to meet Pablo at seven o'clock to go fishing. I had never been a fisherman, but it was time to learn. I wanted to have some relationship with that bountiful sea, some involvement more profound than merely admiring it from our porch. Besides, I had discovered at Mrs. Gomez's table the incomparable flavor of fresh fish.

I walked the mile over to Bocana, where Pablo keeps his boat. He was waiting for me with a small boy who turned out to be his son, Guillermo. There is always a small boy along when men do their work in Baja. It is the oldest form of apprenticeship.

Guillermo was one of Pablo's four children, the oldest being a boy of fourteen. Pablo and his wife and the children live in the valley just up the road from the store. Their house is up the hill away from the road, a makeshift hovel pieced together by Pablo from scrap lumber, crates, tarpaper, and adobe. There is an adobe oven in the center that serves as a cooking range as well as giving heat in winter. It seems a small house for such a big man and such a big family, but then Pablo is out on the sea a good part of the day, and perhaps it is enough. Every weekday morning the children wait by the road in their freshly laundered clothing for the old yellow bus that takes them, like all the other children in the valley, to the one-room schoolhouse near the highway. Pablo's establishment includes the usual automobile carcass, chickens, and when he is rich, a pig or two. The squalor is camouflaged, as it is everywhere in the valley, by bougainvillaea and geraniums and daisies, and the color of the wash hung out in the sun.

The sea is Pablo's source of income. It provides the fish for his table and for trading with the farmers of the valley for beans and chiles. On weekends he takes Americans out fishing in his boat, for a few dollars, and when there is a good catch he sells some to the other Americans who come down to camp at Bocana but not to fish. He has a battered old Ford. With his boat, it constitutes his estate.

Pablo told me to get into the boat and then he and Guillermo shoved it out over a log and into the surf. The boy hopped in and Pablo heaved at the stern, gaining a few feet with each wave, until at last the boat was off the sand. Then Pablo climbed in and stood at his oars, working us out to water deep enough for the outboard.

He yanked the motor into life and we crept out over the bay. The sea was the color of motor oil. There was some wind and the boat pitched and rolled in the dark swells. A mile from shore Pablo cut the motor and stood in the stern, working the oars to keep the boat steady. He was a fine-looking man, portly but solid, with black hair and a plump face and skin the color you would have if leather could blush. He scanned our surroundings, looking at sea gulls and pelicans and beds of kelp.

"Right here okay," he said, and shipped his oars.

Guillermo baited my hook with anchovy. I knew I was not quite playing the game, allowing a boy to bait my hook. But it was my own apprenticeship, I told myself, as well as his. I dropped the line over the side and reeled it out, all the way to the bottom. The bite came quickly. The rod jumped and bent. In that instant, that first stomach-

tightening sense of engagement and combat with an un-
seen quarry, I was touched fatally by the mystique of
fishing. What Hemingway's prose had failed to do, one
little fish at the bottom of the Bahía Santo Tomás had
done. I was hooked.

The fish on my line, I learned later, was not what
fishermen call a game fish. Still, it was not happy with its
predicament. It had neither the strength nor the disposition of the yellowtail, perhaps, but it was nearly the equal
of the man who had caught it, and I was lucky to bring it
up. Out of the water it thrashed and spun on the line and
Guillermo reached out and pulled it in. It was a fat fish,
strawberry red, perhaps fourteen inches long. Pablo nodded approval. "Rock cod," he said. "Good eating."

I caught two more cod and a whitefish and decided
that was enough. I had no wish to upset the ecology of the
Pacific Ocean my first time out. Besides, I wanted no more
fish than I could eat.

"We go see your house," Pablo said.

He started his motor and turned the boat north,
rounding the points that hide our house from Bocana. We
ran parallel to the shore until finally we stood directly out
from the house, and Pablo worked in through the kelp
beds until we were no more than half a mile offshore.

Against that massive landscape the house seemed in-
significantly small. But even at that distance, with its roof
unfinished, it was handsome, and it seemed in perfect
harmony with its setting. The brick walls glowed in the
early light like the houses of Sorrento, and I saw once
more that Gomez had been right about the Guadalajara
porch.

I was pleased. I knew that however this adventure
might turn out for us personally, we would have done

nothing to blight the Baja landscape. For this, I had to thank Gomez. I had wanted plaster walls and an asphalt roof, because they were cheaper. I was glad he had prevailed. He was right as usual. It was uncanny. Once again the unworthy thought crossed my mind that Gomez had built the house for himself. Oh, well, time would tell. In any case, if it lasted five hundred years, as he had often predicted, it would never be pointed at with shame.

We took the boat back to the mouth of the river and beached it, rolling it up on the log. Pablo cleaned my fish on the beach, cutting out thick white filets and leaving the rest for the sea gulls.

I stopped in at the store for some beer and tortillas and Mrs. Gomez insisted on cooking breakfast for me. I gave up easier than my fish had. I had planned to take the fish back to the house and cook them on the Coleman, but there is an atmosphere about Mrs. Gomez's kitchen, a prevailing warmth and aroma, that makes it hard to leave.

The fish was excellent, a quality which I attributed in some vague way to my skill as a fisherman. Mrs. Gomez served it with tortillas and slices of fresh mango. It was a feast that took me back ten thousand years.

I felt gratified. I had proved that, despite the debilitating strains of urban life, I was still man enough to survive on this savage shore. Of course, Stone Age men had to bait their own hooks and clean their own fish. Or did their women do that, before the liberation? I didn't know. I was only an apprentice primitive.

Stuffed with fish and mango, I set out over the beach and walked under the cliffs until a rocky promontory ran into the surf and blocked my way. I found a gully that looked

easy to climb. Fifty feet up I realized I had got myself into
a difficult spot. I saw no good foothold above me and
going down would not be as easy as coming up.

I looked down at the rocks. What would happen to me
if I fell? Nobody would know. I would lie there alone until
the tide came and washed me out to sea. It seemed to me
the first time since the war that I had felt any sense of
danger, immediate and terrible. I studied the cliff above
me again. It didn't look as bad as I had thought. Perhaps
I had only imagined the danger, just to taste it.

I climbed on, and at the top I found a sandy plateau
with a carpet of succulents, blooming yellow, blue, and
purple. This wild beauty did not seem wild at all, but
exquisitely contrived, like some vast flower arrangement.
Perhaps it really had been arranged, I thought, but it was
not for me to say by whom.

I walked on, oblivious of time. When I got back to
Bocana, it was afternoon. Mrs. Gomez asked me in for
lunch. My recent breakfast notwithstanding, I could not
resist her chicken mole, with spaghetti and meat sauce,
fried tortillas, and chunks of watermelon-red papaya.

I smiled as I remembered how my wife had worried
whether I could make out on my own down here in the
wilderness, miles from the nearest supermarket. As
women do, she underestimated an effete man's latent
drive for survival.

At dusk, when I was beginning to think about dinner,
Pablo came by in his old Ford with some fresh sea bass,
cleaned and ready for the pan. I fried it in Mazola. It was
tender and delicious, and perfectly complemented by the
local wine. I wondered if I could ever adjust to city life
again.

CHAPTER TEN

One afternoon during my bachelor sojourn I drove over to the port to look for excitement. There is more cafe society on Bahía Santo Tomás, I found, than the facilities seem to promise.

The port as usual appeared deserted. The fishermen were out in their boats. The women were not in sight. When I got out of the car three dogs trotted over to check me out, then fell in the road to snooze, too lazy to go back where they had come from.

There was music in the air, though, and it seemed to be coming from the ramshackle *cantina*. It would be a transistor tuned in to Tijuana, I thought at first, but as I walked toward the screen door I realized the sound was live.

I entered. A Mexican woman stood behind the counter tending a few shelves of canned goods, candy, and tobacco. There were crooked tables with battered chairs. A woman who looked American was sitting at one of the tables drinking a bottle of *cerveza*. The eyes of both women were fixed on two men who were evidently attempting to hang a simple one-bulb electric light fixture from the center of the ceiling. At the end of the room two Mexican youths were playing guitars and singing. They were stripped to the waist, and their flesh glistened in the warm room.

I had chanced onto what apparently, for Puerto Santo Tomás, was a festive occasion. There is much respect for the arts and trades in Baja. People love to listen to musicians and watch men at work. This was a double bill.

I walked over to the counter. The storekeeper reluctantly withdrew her gaze from the electricians and fetched me a *cerveza* from an ice box. I took a table and joined the others in watching the show. It turned out to be a two-beer performance. The men were in no hurry, as long as there was *cerveza* and music. They took turns on the ladder, each politely giving the other time to test his own theory as to how it should be done. Meanwhile the musicians sang sadly and passionately of love and betrayal and death, which are the themes of rural music everywhere.

Finally, the fixture was installed, everyone had a last bottle of *cerveza,* and the entertainment was at an end.

Before I left the *cantina* I bought two bottles of *cerveza* and took them back to the house, hoping to have a talk with Gomez. I was in luck. He had come over from the store to work on the pipes under what was to be our kitchen sink. Gomez himself, it turned out, was our plumber.

I opened the *cervezas* and we sat out on the porch in the folding chairs. It was a blameless day, as beautiful as the February day more than a year and a half earlier when my wife and I had first seen the bay.

"Romulo," I said, trying not to sound too inquisitorial, "when are we going to know the actual cost? It keeps going up."

"Don't worry, Jack," he said in his reassuring tone, "we will put it all down in writing."

"We put it down in writing once before," I reminded him.

"That's okay. We will put it down again."

"When?"

"When the time is ripe."

There was no point in that course. I decided to change directions.

"When the house is finished," I said, "if it ever is, how will we know it's ours? You aren't going to give us a deed?"

He laughed, a gentle laugh that expressed not ridicule but a nice appreciation of my humor. "You know, Jack, I can give you no deed. You are not a Mexican. It is against the law. Do you want for you and me to break the law?"

"Of course not, Romulo. You know that. It's just that I want to know—well, you keep saying the house will be ours."

"Of course it is your house."

"How will I know that—when the time is ripe?"

He spread his hands in a gesture that was at once humble and majestic. "I will give you the key."

It was beautiful. I had never admired Gomez more. He had circumvented all the laws and the clerical minds and the petty demands of vain and fearful men and reduced the issue of possession to its one essential. I would have the key. In the eyes of *Dios*, what else mattered?

Sitting there on my Guadalajara porch, sipping my fourth *cerveza* of the afternoon and watching the sea gulls play, I could almost believe it. I wanted to believe it. I saw no reason not to believe it. But then another question crossed my mind like the little rain cloud that was blowing in across Punta Santo Tomás, lonely and ominous.

"When the lease is up," I asked, "how do we know you'll renew it?"

"You have an option."

"No, Romulo. I have read the contract of usufruction very carefully. I don't know what the Spanish copy says. But in *English,* it says very clearly that *you* have the option —Romulo Gomez Monroy—not us."

He shrugged. "Of course that is the law. But I have given you my word. I will give you my option. It is now your option. I am going to renew your lease, Jack, as long as I live."

I hated to go an inch further, but I could hear Dalton's questions in the back of my mind. I had been able to quiet Dalton's doubts, but not my own.

"It isn't that I don't trust you, Romulo," I said. "It's just that, well—my God, people die! Supposing you should die?"

His eyes were sad. He took a sip of *cerveza* and looked out to sea. "We all have to die, Jack," he said at last. "But it is no good to talk about death today. It is too beautiful. Look at the view you are going to have!"

I followed his gaze and saw that the bay was filled with great seagoing Chinese junks, which soon raised their anchors and sailed for Cathay with all my doubts.

That evening Pablo drove over from the valley in his ancient two-tone Ford. Like most cars in Baja, it was a working wreck, a bastard kept alive by parts cannibalized from older wrecks that had given up the ghost. He brought me an armful of firewood and stood in the open door, obviously preparing to say something. His hat was in his hand. It was to be something formal.

"Tomorrow," he said, "you want to go fishing?"

"No, Pablo," I said, "I believe I still have a fish or two left at the store."

"You want some abalone?"

"I'd better wait till Saturday, when my wife comes down."

"Tomorrow," he said, "I will cook a pig."

"Well," I said, not knowing what kind of reaction this news called for.

"My daughter Teresa, she will be seven."

"Oh! It's her birthday."

"*Sí.*"

"That's fine, Pablo," I said, wondering if I had anything to send a seven-year-old girl for a present. "Please tell her happy birthday for me."

"You are coming to the party?"

Teresa's birthday party took place on Friday afternoon after the bus brought the children home from the school at the head of the valley. It was held outside Pablo's house in the shade of a great old live oak. Two long tables had been set up end to end to accommodate the astonishing number of guests who arrived by foot, car, and horseback.

Beer and tequila were flowing freely among the men by the time I arrived, and I was soon raised to the general mood of high spirits. The women had prepared a feast. Guacamole, roasted chicken, fried fish, onions, hot Jalisco peppers, stacks of tortillas, and an enormous bowl of chili and beans which sat at the center of the table and was periodically replenished from steaming pots from the house.

Children were also in great supply. They arrived in

their Sunday garments, solemn as altar boys, but soon their solemnity dissolved and they darted about or hovered over the table like hummingbirds, snatching bits of food and dashing off to their games. Birthday parties must be much the same, I thought, the world over.

Evidently at least three of the women had been assigned by Pablo to make sure that my plate was never empty and my glass never dry. It is true that hot peppers stimulate the appetite for beer, and in what seemed hardly a quarter of an hour I found myself afloat. I was extremely happy. Here I was, eating real Mexican food, outdoors under an oak tree which the padres had passed two hundred years before on their way to the port with their grapes for Spain. This was the real Baja.

Meanwhile, I kept an uneasy eye on the barbecue pit over which, as Pablo had promised, a pig was roasting. This was plainly the main event of the day, and one from which the women were excluded. The men stood around the glowing pit with glazed happy eyes, drinking *cerveza*, shouting jests and watching the little pig sizzle. I wondered if there would be any graceful way to avoid eating the pig when it was served. I have always been suspicious of pork. I had heard those dreadful tales about trichinosis when I was a schoolboy. When I ate roast pig I wanted it burned to a crisp, like the Chinese pig in the fable by Charles and Mary Lamb.

My eye fell on a basket of roast chicken. Perhaps if I stuffed myself on chicken I would be excused from tasting the pig. I reached for a leg and put it between my teeth to take a bite. To my dismay, the leg rejected my incisors. I tried again, using more force. It was incredible. The leg actually seemed to spring back. My mouth flew open. At length I tore off a sliver of this unyielding flesh and slid it back between my molars, where the full strength of my jaws could be brought to bear. The leg was not to be taken by force. Hurriedly, when I wasn't watched, I retrieved it with thumb and finger and dropped it in my plate. I would have to eat the pig.

The pig was excellent. Savory and sweet and tender. I washed it down with raw tequila, and by the time the children cut Teresa's beautiful white cake, surmounted with the word *"FELICIDADES"* in green script, there was not a happier man at the party.

I walked back to the house in the dusk, singing *"La Golondrina"* and feeling both happy and sad, which is how *"La Golondrina"* always makes me feel, like birthday parties and tequila. I was happy for myself and for Teresa. I was sad for the little pig, who would root no more among the geraniums beside the adobe house. And I was sad for the tough old rooster who had given up his life, but not his leg. His voice had heralded its final dawn.

When I woke up the next morning I worried a moment about trichinosis again, but nothing ever happened.

From my porch on Saturday morning I could see Luczynski's Ford van parked by his house. He must have pulled in late the night before. He had his Ford agency in Alhambra, a suburb of Los Angeles, and he usually drove down on Fridays after working hours. I had discovered that Art Luczynski was a handy man to have as a neighbor. He knows how to fix a carburetor or a balky hot water heater and what to do about rust and mice. More important, though, he is a man of amiable disposition and absolutely impervious to worry. He believes there is a practical solution to every problem, from a broken axle to a broken leg.

He is not upset by bad roads, bad weather, or the vagaries of the Mexican law.

Luczynski had started building his house not long after the Millards had started theirs, two years or more ago. He and his wife Wanda had been married after the house was finished. Both had been married before, Luczynski having a married son and Wanda a grown daughter and a son Kenny, who was then about twelve. The two families seemed to have merged congenially, and some weekends they would all come down together, including the wife of Luczynski's son. Some months after the morning I am speaking of, Mrs. Luczynski added an infant son to the household, an event that Luczynski welcomed with his usual equanimity. We had met the Luczynskis at the store, inevitably. We sometimes called on each other, like neighbors everywhere, to borrow salt or see if everything was all right, and young Kenny often rode over on his Honda.

As I surveyed the landscape from our porch that morning I could hear the men at work on our house. It is a pleasant sound, the sound of hammers and saws, especially when you know that the artisans are at work on your own house.

Abel and Sebastían were up on the roof, laying the tile. Salvador was building a cabinet in the kitchen. Sebastían and Salvador were living in the shack behind the house. I thought of them as tenants. Abel was a married man, and lived a mile or so up the valley in an adobe house with his wife and five children. Of the three, only Abel spoke any English, and his was very sparse. My Spanish was still an embarrassment. Beyond *Buenos días* there was little we could say to each other, and once we had said *Buenos días,* that was it for the day. In a way, though, this made our relationship agreeable, if occasionally exasperating. I could watch the men work without belaboring them with questions and advice; they, in turn, could suffer my presence with no obligation to argue or explain. Thus, when Gomez was absent from the scene, the hours passed with smiles and friendly gestures.

All three were competent men, but Salvador worked with a special old-world grace and style. In manner and appearance he made me think of the Don Quixote of classic illustration. Though no longer young, his face was of a patrician beauty, with a handsome nose, bushy gray brows, and a baroque mustache. He was slender as a blade, and in his carpenter's apron, with saw in hand, he looked indeed like the vainglorious don. He was the only Mexican I had seen at Bocana who wore the legendary sombrero, wide of brim and high of crown, and at the sight of a woman, whatever her years, he would sweep it grandly off his head and touch it to his toes. Salvador was a throwback to another Mexico; he was a caballero; and he was a master carpenter, when he was sober, which was most of the time.

In midmorning I saw Luczynski and young Kenny come out of their house, wrestling some large and cumbersome object. The object being removed from the house appeared to be a heavy upholstered chair. If I were given to premonition, I might have sensed then that I was watching the beginning of an event that would in time do much to unsettle my peace of mind.

Luczynski and the boy shoved the chair into the van, then got into the cab and drove up to the road. I assumed they would be going to Bocana. Perhaps the chair had belonged to Gomez, and they were giving it back. The van turned north and trundled over the old road to our house.

"Hi," Luczynski shouted, climbing down from the cab. "How'd you like to have a chair?"

"Fine," I said, hoping it sounded tentative.

He opened the van and horsed the chair out, his boy taking the other end.

"Can't I just help you with that?" I said.

"No problem. We got it. Where do you want it?"

"On the porch would be all right," I said, "for the time being."

They carried the chair up to the porch and dropped it heavily down beside my Thrifty Drug Store chair. I examined it dubiously. It was not a handsome piece of furniture. It had been in use, I guessed, for many years; hard use. It was squarish, and covered in plastic of a dispiriting brown. It tilted to the left.

"It's a recliner," Luczynski said.

"Fantastic."

I sat down in the chair. I felt myself tilt slightly to the left, experiencing a minor disorientation which I quickly found I could correct by tilting my head slightly to the right. Altogether, it wasn't uncomfortable. I pushed back to try the reclining position.

"The recliner doesn't work," Luczynski said. "It's busted inside. I think we could fix it. No problem."

"No, no," I said. "I don't need to recline. I'm just happy to have something comfortable to sit in. Until we get our furniture in, at least. I don't know, of course, how it's going to fit in with my wife's color scheme. But of course we'll let you have it back."

"No problem. We don't need it anymore. When you're done with it, just pass it on to the next fellow. Gomez is starting a new house, I hear. Some guy named Schmidt."

"Well, thanks," I said. "I'd offer you a beer, but of course we don't have our refrigerator yet."

"You've got a gas refrigerator lined up?"

"Not yet. Gomez is going to get one for us."

"Oh," he said. "Well, don't be in any hurry."

CHAPTER ELEVEN

It was Saturday afternoon when my wife arrived from Los Angeles. There was a patch of red tile on the roof. I had watered her oleanders and they looked clean and healthy. There had been no incidents on the road. The day was blameless. She was happy.

"Gomez is going to start another house," I told her.

"He told you that?"

"No. Luczynski."

That is the way news always comes in Baja. It is never transmitted by the source, but always by some second party, one step or more removed. I would talk to Pablo or Luczynski for news of Gomez, and to Gomez for news of Pablo and Luczynski. Sometimes I drove over to the store at the port and learned something about Bocana; and vice versa. No news was ever quite whole or correct in every detail. To verify a story, it was necessary to draw it from at least two other witnesses, and then close in on the irreducible sum of it by triangulation.

It turned out to be true that Gomez was going to start a new house for another American couple, Hal and Shirley Schmidt. Hal Schmidt, Gomez said, was the president of a very substantial, nationwide financial corporation with its home office in Los Angeles. It was momentous news, as there were only two houses besides our own, and the new one would be a one-third increase in the population of our little colony. Also, I felt somehow reassured. If a successful financier was going to build at Bocana, he must have made a thorough investigation and found everything in order. My worries had been groundless.

That evening in the store I asked Gomez about the Schmidt house again. "It is going to be a very big house," he explained. "Twice as big as yours."

"If you start a new house, how can you finish ours?"

"Don't worry, Jack, the new house, it is going to take some time. First we must go to Ensenada for the lease, and then we must change the road."

"You're going to change the road again?"

"Of course."

The sky looked uncertain that night, and I thought it would be best to stay in the cabin at Bocana, but it was rented. We slept in the house on the folding cots. The wind came up, blowing through the open doors and down the unfinished fireplace and playing tunes in the new roof tiles. Gomez had built us an organ.

Sometime after midnight we were wakened by a frightful racket. The wheeze and clatter of an ancient car. Men laughing and singing. The glare of headlights in the house. The hollow slamming of a plywood door.

"What is it?" Denny whispered.

"It's our tenants," I said. "They must have gone to Ensenada. It's Saturday night, you know."

The weather had failed to make good on its threats, and in the morning the sky was clear and the wind bland. We stood on the porch and surveyed our estate. New growth had already taken over the old road that now abutted on the north side of the house. The desert was coming back. Even the earth Gomez had scraped clean for the house was burgeoning again with enormous tumbleweeds.

Denny said, "I've got to get out next time and cut those back."

"Forget it," I said. "You can't fight the whole desert."

We were going to have breakfast at the store, but I heated water and made coffee and she went out to water her oleanders. She was back in a moment.

"There's no water in the hose. Not a drop."

"Is it necessary?"

"I think they ought to be watered. They look a little peaked."

"I'll do what I can."

I drove up to the reservoir. That was the first step. I didn't want to tell Gomez the reservoir was empty until I was sure. I parked and walked up to the window and swung the shutter open and looked down into the tank. Ten feet below me the surface of the water shone in the filtered light. It appeared to be only inches above the bottom, too low to flow through the outlet and down through the plastic pipe to our house.

Something in the water caught my eye; a movement, quick and shiny. I strained to make it out in the fanciful light. It was a little frog; alive and kicking.

The time had come to propitiate our god. I got in the car and drove down to the store. It was too early for the store to be open, but I knew Gomez was there. All four of his dogs were waiting by the kitchen door. Gomez was in the kitchen pounding abalone.

"*Buenos días, señor,*" he said. His face was beatific this morning. It might have been painted by Rembrandt, it seemed so full of character and light. *"Cómo está usted?"*

"Muy bien," I said, "but we have no water."

"And your wife? She is fine this beautiful morning?"

"Sí, she is fine. But she has no water, for her plants."

"No water?"

"Yes, no water. The reservoir is dry."

"It is dry?"

"Almost. I just looked."

Gomez shrugged. "No use to worry, Jack. We fill it up."

It seemed like an opportune moment to settle the question of the source. I still had in mind the morning I had found the water truck drinking from the lagoon instead of the well.

"Where does it really come from, Romulo?" I asked.

"The water?"

"Yes."

He spread his hands palms up. "The water, *señor,* it comes from God. We just have to do a little dance. That's all."

I knew I would never ask him again.

"By the way," I said, "you've got a frog in your reservoir."

"A frog?" His face fell. "The little frog is drowned?"

"Not at all. He's very much alive."

"Ah," said Gomez. "That is good. *Gracias a Dios.*"

Later we saw the old water truck crawling up the hill toward the reservoir. Gomez's dogs were loping along beside it. In time the water came. There was air in the pipes, though, and when the water came through, it made a little sound, like a frog croaking.

Monday morning we started back to Los Angeles, feeling foolish to be taking two cars. It would have been more foolish, though, to leave one car behind. It might stand idle for weeks.

There was no point in one of us following the other, since we both knew the way and following is dangerous, but I started out directly behind my wife, dropping off far enough to avoid her dust.

When I reached the paved road I caught up and followed her into Ensenada. Over the past few miles my brake had begun to soften. It was a worrisome symptom, with two hundred miles of high-speed freeway yet ahead. I decided to overtake her and ask her to wait till I found out what was wrong. Then the pedal went alarmingly spongy. I let the car slow down and gave the brake another pump. It firmed up, then sank slowly to the floor, and the car rolled on. With a feeling of desolation I saw her dusty red Mustang disappear in the traffic on the Calle Primera. She was gone beyond recall. I was in trouble.

I slipped down into low gear and crept along. At the first corner I turned into an unpaved street. It was gouged and pitted, exactly what I needed to help me stop. A block ahead I saw a garage. I crawled up to the entrance and started to turn in, but a man ran out and blocked my way, waving his arms.

"Ford–Chevy!" he shouted, shaking his head at my little French bonbon. "Ford–Chevy!"

I understood. For years the transport of Baja had survived by the interchangeability of parts. The Ford and the Chevrolet were standard. The peninsula was strewn with their carcasses, but not a part was wasted. Every detachable organ was cannibalized and put back into the mainstream. A Dodge might even make it; but a Renault was something else. It might as well have been a Maxwell or an Essex as far as this mechanic was concerned.

"*Donde?*" I shouted out the window, holding up my hands in the sign language of helplessness. "Where can I go?"

He came to the car and indicated that I should go to the second corner, turn left, and go two blocks. I backed cautiously into the street and started out at a crawl, saving my fading brakes for the final stop.

The place he had sent me to, praise *Dios,* was a brake shop. I inched in and pushed my brake. It gave its final thrust, like a spent old man. The car stopped. A young man came out of an office smiling. "Yes, sir," he said. How beautiful it was, the sound of English.

His name was Octavio. He got in the car and tried the brake. "It is the master cylinder," he said. He could repair it, yes; but he would have to send to San Diego for the parts. There were no Renault parts in Baja; he knew that for a fact.

"San Diego?" I said. "How long will it take?"

"I will see my agent tonight," he said, the word agent making it sound conspiratorial. "He goes to San Diego tomorrow. Tomorrow night he comes back. The next day, your car is ready."

That meant two days and two nights. I would be stranded in Ensenada. My wife was beyond reach, speeding home. There was no phone to Bocana. I checked my wallet; only $13 in cash. Oh, well. I could stay at the Hotel Bahía on my credit cards. The prospect wasn't altogether depressing. I had heard that the Bahía was where the action was in Ensenada, and they said the floor show was a lulu.

"Go ahead," I told Octavio. "I'll see you in two days."

I walked toward the center of town, thinking I would find a *cantina* and have a *cerveza* to cheer me up. The most engaging of cities turns cold when a man is stranded and short of money. On the Avenida Ruiz I turned into a small café. It was a place we had never been; only a hole in the wall, in a part of town few tourists would seek out. But I was drawn through the open door by the aroma of tortillas. I was hungry.

I sat at a bare wooden table and examined a dog-eared menu. There was only one other patron in the place, a woman sitting at the counter. It occurred to me that she was an American woman, and she looked familiar. For a split second I didn't recognize her. Then she turned and looked in my direction.

"My God," I said. "What are you doing here?"

It was one of those fantastic coincidences that may happen two or three times in a lifetime; too improbable for fiction; so improbable that you feel a sense of infinite mystery, and wonder about it for years to come.

I fell silent as we sped homeward over the freeway in her car.

"What are you thinking about?" she asked. "What it was that caused us both to pick that funny little café back there?"

"Yes," I said, "I guess that was it."

It wasn't though. What I was really thinking about was the action I was going to miss that night at the Bahía.

The next afternoon I tried to phone Octavio from Los Angeles to see if his agent had got the part. The circuits were busy, a common occurrence between Los Angeles and Baja. An hour later I got through.

"*Bueno,*" said a voice at the other end.

"*Bueno,*" I said. "This is Jack Smith, in Los Angeles. The man who left the Renault."

"*Bueno?*"

"*Bueno?*"

"*Bueno.*"

It turned out to be a wrong number.

I tried once more and got through to Octavio.

"Ah, yes," he said. "Mr. Smith."

"You have the part?"

"No. We do not have it yet."

He had made contact with his agent the night before, as planned, and the man had left for San Diego.

"But he does not come back," Octavio said.

The next morning I phoned again.

"Ah, yes," said Octavio. "He could not get the part in San Diego. Today he goes to La Mesa."

I felt like Sydney Greenstreet, the employer of a network of secret agents, slipping over international borders in the furtherance of my interests. But I doubted that La Mesa would prove any more fruitful than San Diego. I asked Octavio whether he would mind if I procured the master cylinder in Los Angeles, and took it down to Ensenada myself.

"*Bueno,*" he said. "I will tell my agent in La Mesa."

I bought the cylinder and we drove down Saturday morning. When we entered Ensenada I was absorbed in looking for the side street to the brake shop and wasn't watching what I was doing. Suddenly a policeman stepped out in front of us and motioned me sternly to the curb.

"Oh, God," I sighed. "What have I done!"

"You went through an *Alto* sign, for one thing," said Denny. "*Alto* means stop, you know."

"Damn," I muttered. "I keep thinking it means high."

We had never had an accident and never been stopped by a policeman in Baja. I was not inclined to believe all the tales I had heard about being taken off to jail for a minor violation, or at best haled before a venal magistrate to pay an exhorbitant fine. Even so, I dreaded the day one of us might have to put our skepticism to the test. Arrest was the event I most wished to avoid, short of murder, snakebite or a broken leg.

The policeman marched around the front of the car, giving us a good look at his immaculate brown uniform, and leaned into the window on my side, scowling. He was a picture of authority with his Sam Browne belt and his badge and pistol.

"I'm sorry," I told him. "Pardon. I keep thinking *alto* means high. It means high in English, you know."

He put his ticket book down on the door. I was resigned. We would be able to laugh, I hoped, when it was all over.

"One dollar," the policeman said.

One dollar? It was cheap enough, whatever I had done. But I was surprised and rather disappointed. It was true then, what we had heard about the roadside fines, that they were nothing less than bribes.

Quickly, before the price went up, I slipped a dollar from my wallet and handed it out the window, folded twice. The policeman handed me a ticket.

"*Buenos días,*" he said, and backed away with a half-salute.

I passed the ticket over to Denny and drove on, alert for every sign and hazard.

"*Baile Anual,*" she said, reading from the ticket. "*Baile Anual de los elementos de Transito Municipal, el dia 20 Noviembre a las 21 horas en el Salon de los Cristales, La Orquestra de Mike Dial. Coca-Cola! Refresca en grande!"*

"*Baile?*" I said. "*Baile?* Doesn't that mean dance?"

"You just bought a ticket," she said, "for the annual Policemen's Ball."

I delivered the master cylinder to Octavio and we decided to leave the Renault overnight and drive on down to Bocana in the Mustang. As long as we were that close, it would be foolish not to go the rest of the way and look in on the house.

The dirt road was in good shape. It showed signs of having been graded recently, and here and there, in an especially smooth-looking stretch, I let the speedometer creep up to 35 mph, feeling safe.

I have called the road bad. That is a relative term. For people familiar with the truly bad roads of Baja, it is a very good road. This is due not to chance but to the presence of the cement plant down on the coast beside the airstrip. The men who work at the plant have families in Ensenada, and the company sends them home on weekends by bus. Thus, it is incumbent on the company to keep the road passable, lest the morale of its employees suffer.

But passable too is a relative term. The company depends a great deal on the mettle of its bus and driver, and thus it can afford to ignore certain refinements that would be an aid to those with less experience and skill.

For example, the company has never troubled to repair the broken cattleguard that lies athwart the road at about the halfway point. It is a simple sort of makeshift guard, its purpose being to prevent cows from crossing from one pasture to another through the break in the fence necessitated by the road. A gate would be too much trouble to open and close, so the guard is merely a trench dug across the road and covered with lengths of iron pipe. The pipes allow cars to pass over the ditch, but cows don't find the footing to their liking and won't attempt it. However, the guard has become a treacherous trap for the uninitiated motorist. On one side the pipes have long since caved in, so that a car must keep to the left going in and the right coming out, or drop one wheel into the gap.

We had learned to anticipate the cattleguard from certain landmarks, especially a magnificent oak tree stump that stood nearby. The sound procedure was to slow down, bear to the good side, and creep across the clanking hollow pipes of the cattleguard with a prayer. But this Saturday the cattleguard was not in my mind as we rumbled over the road, and when we came to the tree its message failed to reach me.

Denny shouted, "The cattleguard!"

I hit the brake; too late. We skidded up on the cattleguard and the right front wheel sank into the hole with a sound like a train wreck.

Utter silence fell. It was a minute before I could move. Then we got out to appraise our predicament. The wheel had not only sunk into the hole, but the tire had blown. The car was much too heavy for us to lift out. We would have to wait for help. One thing was in our favor. No one could pass until we were out of the way.

For a man conditioned to city life there is no loneliness like that of a deserted road on which his car breaks down. The silence enveloped us. Our dust soon settled and then there was no movement. Nothing stirred. In both directions the road was empty. We were alone on earth.

"We might as well sit in the shade," I said.

"I hope you aren't having another heart attack."

We walked down the road to a cottonwood tree and sat in the shade. Gradually, the subtle sounds of the valley began to penetrate the silence. A whir of wings, a crow's call, a distant cow. Finally there was a faint drumming, in and out at first, perhaps an illusion; then firmer, and coming on. In a minute there was no doubt. It was an engine. We got up and stood beside the car, looking helpless.

The sound grew to a roar and a plume of dust arose above the road to the west. In a moment the source of this beneficent intrusion appeared at the crest of a rise and lumbered toward us. It was the cement company's Saturday bus.

The bus pulled up abruptly on the far side of the cattleguard. The doors flew open. Out came the passengers, a dozen of them, leaping down to the ground and trotting toward us, laughing and shouting and waving their arms like boys taking a soccer field. Without stopping to inspect the problem, they crowded around the front end of the Mustang, jostling for a grip on the bumper. Seeing what was required of me, I jumped into the car and started it up. The men shouted together and straightened their backs. The wheel came out. I shoved the car in reverse and backed it away from the cattleguard.

How could I thank them? There was no time. They trotted back to the bus. I ran after them. The door slammed shut. Laughing faces appeared at the windows. I took off my hat, and like Salvador, I brushed the brim across my toes. The bus rumbled on across the cattleguard and vanished in its own dust.

Inspired by this spontaneous act of chivalry, I changed the wheel without complaint, and we were soon on our way. It was not, however, to be our last adventure of the day.

Some distance short of the fork, where the main road goes off to the cement plant and the lesser to Bocana, we came upon an unfamiliar obstruction. There was a makeshift barricade of logs and boulders across the road, and a detour had been plowed by tires around to the right. At dead center of the road beyond the barricade stood a rickety well rig, and off at a distance a heavy-duty generator, thrashing away.

"What is it?"

"It's a water well," I said. "Somebody's digging a water well in the middle of the goddamn road. What *arrogance!*"

The detour was a trap; deep powdery dust that had not yet had a chance to pack. I ground into it with trepidation, and was halfway in before I had that sickening certainty that one more turn of the wheels and we would be stuck. Slowly, trying not to spin, I backed out over my tracks. I got out and surveyed the terrain. The only way was to blaze a new route where there was still a crust on the ground. We crunched slowly through brush and over rocks, looping around the new establishment and connecting once more with the road.

"If it rains," I said, "we'll never get out."

CHAPTER TWELVE

The store at Bocana was closed, so we headed for the house. We had gone only half a mile, though, when we came to a barricade, and a red arrow crayoned on a piece of cardboard pointed out a detour.

"He's moved the road again," I said incredulously, though it was perfectly obvious.

The new road went higher up the hillside, looping around the old one. As we climbed over it we looked down on the bypassed portion of the old road and saw a familiar sight. A plot of ground had been scraped bare across the old road, evidently in preparation for a new house.

"What arrogance," Denny said. I wasn't sure whether she meant it or whether she was merely mocking me.

There were three men on the site and one of them was in khaki, with a Panama hat. It was Gomez. The site was hardly more than a quarter-mile from ours. It was between the Luczynski house and the Millard house, so that when the house was built we would be able to see all three. Our community was growing.

"You have moved the road again," I said to Gomez as soon as we had completed the customary compliments.

"Oh, yes," he said. "It was necessary. Otherwise, everybody would be running into this house."

I thought it over. There was nothing to say. It was a kind of logic that lay safely beyond argument.

"Somebody's digging a well in the valley," Denny said, "in the middle of the road."

His expression hardened. "Those guys," he said, "they got a lot of nerve."

As usual when he was irritated he used American slang. It was evident, as he spoke of the well, that he regarded digging a well in a road as at least rude, and perhaps a disruption of the divine scheme.

"It is a pain in the neck."

From the size of the clearing I could see that the new house was to be grander than ours.

"How can you build two houses at once," I asked him, "with your little crew?"

"Don't worry, Jack, your house comes first. I am only preparing the land."

"When you finish this one," I said, "I guess our house will no longer be your masterpiece."

"Jack," said Gomez, "this house can't take away your view."

He was right. Gomez had given us our view, and only Gomez could take it away.

"You will come to dinner tonight?" he asked, gentle again. "I am going to cook some lobster for you."

When we arrived at the store that evening, Mrs. Gomez and Marisa were in the kitchen preparing dinner.

"Romulo is not here?" I said.

"He is up there," said Mrs. Gomez, pointing to the top of the knoll where Gomez's cabins stood, "working on the generator. Any excuse, you know, Jack, to stay out of the kitchen. There is nothing wrong with the generator."

"He has a gift for fixing machines," I said.

"Yes, that is true. But I am not going to cook the lobster." She was smiling, but there was great strength in Mrs. Gomez's smile.

"I am not either," said Marisa. For a Mexican housewife and daughter, I suspected, this was a substantial rebellion.

We were having a cup of coffee when Gomez arrived. He was carrying a gunny sack from which he drew a large live lobster.

"Buenas noches," he said, and walked to the sink where Marisa was patting tortillas. She uttered a squeak and turned her back as he dropped the lobster into the sink.

"He is a beauty," Gomez said.

"I will put the water on," said Mrs. Gomez, "and that is all."

While the pot heated Gomez poured tequila.

"To your newest house," I said, thinking to be gracious.

"To your mansion," said Gomez.

When the pot was boiling Gomez lifted the lobster and held it for an instant in the steam, taking aim. The lobster worked its joints this way and that, groping for a way out of its unpromising predicament. Gomez dropped it in. The lobster relaxed and sank silently out of sight.

Mrs. Gomez had turned her head away, her face suffused with a lofty wry detachment. "They don't *like* it, you know," she told us confidentially.

Gomez quickly reached into the sack and pulled out a smaller lobster, which he added to the pot, and then another.

"One time," he said "I used to ship these lobsters to the Orient."

"The Orient?" I said. "Where in the Orient?"

"Oh, Japan and Hong Kong."

"But Romulo," I said, remembering what he had told us the day we met, "you said you shipped them to the United States. It was your contribution to the war effort."

"Oh, yes," he said, "but after the war, I shipped them to Japan and Hong Kong."

He had driven the lobsters up through the two Californias to San Francisco, and from there they were flown to their destinations.

Hong Kong! It seemed fantastic that this little bay on a forgotten peninsula should have had a commercial link with the Orient. But then I remembered the Chinese junks that had put in here for abalone a century and more ago.

I realized that I had never liked or trusted any man more than Gomez, but he remained mysterious and elusive. He had done many things, I suspected, to survive on this arid peninsula, which had lured and destroyed so many adventurers. He did not talk freely about the past, but now and then the curtain would part for a moment, revealing some graphic scene, like a clip from an old Humphrey Bogart movie.

There was the time a rattlesnake got into the pilot's cabin of a small plane and lay coiled at his feet as he and the pilot sweated out a mission over the Baja mountains. The pilot's name had been Cervantes. What the cargo had been, Gomez never said.

"You have done many things," I said.

"Oh, yes. I have had no choice. And still I have no choice." He turned to us with a smile that was both sweet and enigmatic. "Maybe someday I will have my reward."

I laughed. Had he meant our house? He knew what I was thinking. He laughed too. I think of it as my private joke, that Gomez really built our house for himself. But Gomez always laughs, too. He is the most polite of men.

In two weeks Gomez telephoned us at our home in Los Angeles. We had learned by then that when he phoned he was in need of money, though of course he never mentioned it. We had long since abandoned the payment scheme called for in our contract, and had been sending Gomez whatever we could, to keep him going and to avoid those staggering lump sums.

"*Buenos días,*" he began.

"*Buenos días.*"

"*Cómo está usted?*"

"*Muy bien. Y usted?*"

"*Muy bien, gracias. Y su esposa?* Your wife? Denny?"

As always, he was sensitive to my lack of Spanish, slipping graciously into English when he sensed that the conversation had exhausted my vocabulary.

"She is all right," I said. "And Delia?"

"*Muy bien,*" said Gomez. "She is fine. And your family? Your sons? They are all right?"

"They are fine. And how is your family? They are well?"

"My family is all right. And you, *señor.* You are well?"

"I'm fine. What is it, Romulo? Are you having trouble?"

"The roof, *señor,* it is finished."

"Wonderful! We must send you some money, then."

"It is up to you, *señor.* There is no hurry."

"How does it look, Romulo, with the roof finished?"

"It is beautiful, my friend. Many people see your house, they say it is the most beautiful house in Bocana."

"Well, of course there are only the other two."

"It is a mansion."

"I'll try to send you some money next week. Will that be soon enough?"

"As you wish. It is time to pick out the tile."

That was exciting, the thought of picking out the tile. It meant we were nearing the end. The tile would be the final touch. We had looked forward to picking it out. The ceramic tiles of Mexico are unsurpassed for vivacity of color and design.

"Good, Romulo. When can we do that?"

"Saturday," he said, "I am all day in Tijuana."

We agreed to meet at ten o'clock in the Hotel Caesar, on the Avenida Revolución.

"What did he want?" my wife asked when I hung up.

"He wanted to know how we are."

We drove down to San Diego Friday to spend the night and crossed the border early. We didn't want to be late.

Tijuana is a hustling town. Like a girl who once worked in a bordello, she has a bad reputation that won't fade. And she certainly has been naughty. How can a working girl remain chaste when she's just across the border from the U.S. Pacific Fleet?

Even at nine o'clock of a Saturday morning the pitchmen are out in front of the girlie joints with their flashlights, beckoning passersby into those dark caves where girls dance naked on the bar; street urchins gang up on your car, promising to guard it from each other for a nickel; taxi drivers hang around the good hotels like bees around a mescal bloom, ready to take you to the American consulate or a house full of almost-virgins, take your choice, for $1.50.

On the other hand, Tijuana is probably safer than

most American cities, especially after dark. Its long main street, the Avenida Revolución, is lively and clean. Its arcades and open-air bazaars are gorged with Mexican handmade goods: suede jackets, cowhide boots and holsters, wrought iron lamps and wine racks, embroidered shirts, silver bracelets and turquoise rings, onyx chess sets, paper flowers. Some of it is sleazy, some of it is wonderful, and all of it is negotiable.

The mariachi in their spangled costumes fill the arcades with music, happy and sad; a hundred little kitchens give off the odors of beans, beer, and tortillas. The shopkeepers are amiable and gallant, and willing to bargain themselves into poverty, to please the American lady.

For the affluent and sophisticated, the avenida offers quality import stores like those on the best streets of Rome, London, and Paris; quiet, air-conditioned carpeted shops whose chic saleswomen do not deign to haggle, but may grant the house discount to bona fide customers. Tijuana is a free city; thus, genuine bargains are to be found in haute couture, Italian gloves, French perfumes, Spanish porcelain, or Belgian lace.

The Hotel Caesar is neither large nor pretentious, and it is no longer "the place" with the American bullfight crowd. Modern motels and the palatial Azteca have rendered it declassé. In its decline, though, it has taken on an old-world charm and a dignity that are distinctly Mexican. It was here, in the kitchens of Caesar's Grill, that Caesar first concocted his famous salad, and here it is still prepared at table by red-jacketed waiters with the style of matadors.

Gomez was exactly on time, but he had made no other adjustments to the demands of the city. He wore the familiar boots, khakis, and Panama hat. He was a working man in a working city. Yet there was nothing about him of the rube.

"You would like a little tequila?" he asked, turning a hand toward the bar.

"Afterward," I said. "Let's get on with it."

I had a sense of intrigue. We were, after all, keeping a rendezvous with an elusive foreigner in a notorious international city. Our mission was merely the selection of tiles for the house, but Gomez as usual had managed to color it with mystery and excitement by the sheer magic of his presence.

"Come with me," he said, and we fell into step, taking a side street off the Avenida Revolución. The tile shop was two blocks away. Its displays were proliferous and dazzling. It was the sort of bonanza that could engage my wife for hours, if not days. Time only reinforces her indecision when she is confronted with such a wealth of choices. In an hour I was hopelessly confused and taut with impatience. The colors had all begun to run together. Gomez was serene.

"There is no hurry," he told her for the hundredth time. "Your tile will last five hundred years."

At last we agreed on a blue and yellow tile for the bathroom, a dark blue, mauve, and yellow for the bartop, and a pale green, yellow, and ocher for the kitchen. Gomez had suggested blue for the kitchen too, instead of green, pointing out that then it would match the bar.

"No, the house is full of blue already," Denny said. "I think a touch of green will be refreshing."

"Of course," said Gomez, "you are right."

"I wonder if I can just buy a single tile of each pattern," she said, "so I can match the colors."

The tiles were available at twenty-five cents apiece,

and in the end she bought six and slipped the brown
paper sack into her bag.

We walked back to the Caesar and sat at the bar for a
drink of tequila.

"To the house," I said.

"To your mansion," said Gomez.

Denny said, "Romulo, how long will it be now?"

"Your house will be finished," said Gomez, "in two
months."

Two months? Not three? It was a breakthrough.

In the dark bar Gomez told us quietly how to get back
across the border without a long wait in line. The U.S.
government's Operation Intercept was then in effect, an
intensive drive against drug smuggling, and the delay was
sometimes hours. Gomez advised us to drive to Tecate, a
much smaller and less traveled border town thirty-two
miles east of Tijuana. At Tecate there would be no heavy
traffic, and the crossing would be quick.

We parted company with Gomez and drove to Tecate
through the stony brown hills and turned north at the
town plaza, as instructed. The border was two blocks
away, and as Gomez had predicted, the gate was clear.

The customs inspector leaned to look into the car.
"You are American citizens?"

"Yes."

"What did you buy in Mexico?"

"Nothing. We were only down for an hour or two."

He wasn't satisfied. Something bothered him. Perhaps
it was my wife. Sometimes a perfectly innocent woman
looks guilty. He looked into our suitcase and her overnight bag and in the trunk and under the hood. At Tijuana
we had never been subjected to such a thorough search.

"All right," he said at last. "You can go on." But he
didn't sound too sure.

A minute later, as the border fell away behind us, Denny clapped a hand to her cheek.

"Oh, my," she said, holding up the brown paper sack with her sample tiles.

We were international smugglers.

CHAPTER THIRTEEN

"Let's take the Airedale this time," I suggested one day when we were packing.

"Won't we need some papers to get him back across the border?"

"There's something about rabies," I said. "I'll find out."

I telephoned the U.S. Public Health Service at the border and asked what would be required. All we needed, a woman told me, was a veterinarian's certificate that the dog had been innoculated against rabies within the past two years. We had that.

"What about getting him *into* Mexico?" I asked. "Do we need anything for that?"

"That's a good question. You'd better check with the Mexican Consulate in San Diego."

I phoned the consulate. "Yes," a woman told me. "You must get a health certificate from your veterinarian."

I would have to present the certificate at the consulate, in duplicate. One copy would be stamped and returned to me. It would be good for one year. The fee would be four dollars.

It seemed sensible. Mexico was certainly as wise to protect itself from our mad dogs as we were from theirs.

I drove the Airedale down to the dog and cat hospital and got the health certificate in duplicate.

By then, though, it was too late to reach the consulate in San Diego during business hours. We decided to wait overnight and start out early. It was a nuisance, but the time had come to give the dog a try.

I had bought him as a pup, specifically with the idea of taking him with us to Baja as companion and watchdog. He was an Airedale of blameless pedigree. He was handsome, brave, and intelligent, and I had never known an animal, man or beast, with a greater zest for mischief.

For six months he visited one calamity upon us after another. He shredded nylons, furniture, and magazines without discrimination. He learned to whirl the lazy Susan cupboard in the kitchen, just for the joy of hearing the clatter of pots and pans as they spun out on the floor. He polka-dotted the living room carpet, and industriously altered the entire back yard, uprooting and burying with random abandon.

Now at last he had emerged from his reckless adolescence. He was buoyant as ever, but not as destructive. His intelligence was uncanny; his character exemplary. I have never believed the message of those sentimental dog stories, that people can learn character from dogs. Perhaps there is no harm in the idea that dogs can teach us patience, loyalty, and courage, among other virtues, but a dog is a dog and a man is a man, and they have different kinds of patience, loyalty, and courage; and what may conceivably be a virtue in one is not even logical in the other. Who can imagine a chaste dog?

He was mature, and I was eager to take him from his fenced yard and turn him loose on our boundless landscape down in Baja.

"I'll bet," Denny said, "that the Mexicans don't even ask about him at the border."

I knew she might be right. But it was a chance I could never take. I have my own kind of daring, but I have no stomach for those checkpoint confrontations. I don't like the suspense—that crucial moment when the guard bends down to peer inside and it's life or death. I've sat through it too many times in Hitchcock movies. There is never any contraband in my luggage; no forgery in my papers, no falseness in my story. I like to cross clean.

It was the Airedale's first long trip. He was a jewel. He traveled exactly like my wife. Once he understood that we weren't just going down to the supermarket and back he settled down and fell asleep.

The air in San Diego was clear and clean. The woman at the Mexican consulate was pretty and polite. My annoyance at this trying red tape vanished. With the pink certificate in hand, stamped officially and good for a year, I walked back to the car and we headed for the border.

There was hardly any traffic going in. The dog had awakened when the car slowed down and was standing up in the back seat, eminently visible. We crept into the gate. The guard eyed us. His face was unreadable.

"Go ahead," I taunted, trying mental telepathy on him, "ask us for his papers."

The guard's eyes moved back to the car behind us. There was the slightest jerk of his head. He was through with us. I drove on. It was exasperating, to have wasted all that time on a needless detail. But in my heart I knew we had done the right thing. We had acted with honor. It is the only way to raise a dog.

It is possible to spend a whole day at our house in Baja without catching sight of another human being, except for someone going by on the road to the port or a fisherman out on the bay in a boat.

I keep thinking that in this isolation I may one day be the instrument of a divine insight, one of those profound flashes that change men's lives.

Perhaps it is only a myth that great thoughts are engendered by solitude. Perhaps they are just as likely to come at cocktail parties or in crowded elevators; but then they are lost, because you can't write them down. There isn't enough elbow room.

I did have my moment down on the beach, when it came to me about Random Chance. But nothing of comparable magnitude has ever struck me since, and I am unable to say for sure that any advantages have ever come to me from that experience itself.

Sitting on the porch with the Airedale one morning, though, I was favored by a look into primitive instincts of a kind that are rarely perceived in the city.

First I observed that the dog was behaving in an extraordinary way. He was standing stiff, like a pointer, tilted slightly forward, and he was inching ahead, one exquisitely cautious step at a time, lifting each paw an inch or two and setting it softly down. I had never seen him act with such restraint. His habit is to leap at anything that is warm.

I followed the line of his gaze. My pulse quickened. A roadrunner stood on the wall of the porch, his tail turned to the dog. He didn't look quite full-grown himself. Like the dog, he had not yet fulfilled the promise of his genes. He was still an immature bird, awkward and uncertain, and he was in peril.

I held my breath as the dog closed the distance and the roadrunner grew increasingly tense, jerking his head this way and that, searching for whatever impalpable danger it was that was making him so uneasy. The suspense tightened with every step the dog took.

I was tempted to intercede; to take this drama out of the hands of Random Chance and into my own. All I had to do was shout, and the bird would fly. Omnipotence is appealing. But then I remembered the turban snail, and how I had felt after popping him into the lovely beige stomach of the sea anemone.

As I temporized the crisis was resolved. Suddenly the bird scooted along the wall away from the dog. The dog bounded foolishly after him, abandoning grace and stealth, knowing the game was up. The bird glided down from the wall and vanished in the tumbleweeds. He hadn't needed me after all.

It was midmorning when the pelicans came. There were fifty or sixty of them, gliding over the bay in formation, low and slow, evidently hunting down a school of fish. With terrible suddenness they would peel off and drop to the water, hurtling straight down, their awesome bills aimed like swords, dropping as if their aerodynamic characteristics had suddenly been canceled, striking like projectiles. Gomez had called them the Mexican Air Force, and indeed they did resemble attacking dive bombers in old film clips of World War II.

The show was just beginning. Evidently they had spotted a sizable feast about a quarter-mile out from our porch. Soon they were joined by a flight of sea gulls, smaller and quicker, like fighter planes among the bombers. Then came the cormorants, flying low and fast, as if executing a timely counterattack. They splashed down en masse, blackening the water.

Water and sky were athrash with screaming birds. The attack was in full fury when a new element entered the theater of action. First I saw a silken dark gray curve above the water, topped by a fin, and then another. Two porpoises had joined the fray.

For ten minutes the slaughter continued, until it seemed that the birds would be exhausted, or too full to fly. Then gradually the scene moved out toward the open sea. The fish had regrouped their tattered formation and rallied to escape the dreadful trap. Squadron by squadron the glutted birds departed for their bases.

Random Chance had blown the whistle. The sport was over. All was serene.

We had the seashore almost to ourselves. I had seen three Americans down on the pebble beach—a youth and two girls—but they had struck their little camp one morning and trundled off over the dirt road in their green Volkswagen, pulling a ball of dust along behind them like a bustle, and I supposed they had gone for good.

Night and day had been warm. A hot wind blew over the point and across the bay, riding up and over the cliffs and wrecking itself against our house like a train. From our porch we could see the shacks of the port, white as bones on the dark point. We knew there were people at the port, but no straining of the eyes would make them visible from our house.

Late in the afternoon I struck out with the Airedale for a walk along the pebble beach. I imagined us quite alone.

We took the ramp that goes down through a deep gully to the beach. Cars with good traction can make it down and up again, but I was surprised to see the green Volkswagen down at the bottom and near it a light camp set out around a spread-out blanket. I heard shrill cries and saw the three campers out in the surf, blond hair and fair skin flashing in the late sun. Ah, youth, to frolic in the winter sea!

The dog and I walked on up the beach a quarter of a mile or so. The tide was out and the beach was broad and flat. We trotted along the wet sand, splashing in the icy waves, and then the dog saw something far up the beach and made for it at a gallop.

I shouted vainly in the wind and ran after him. He had joined two children in blue swimsuits, a girl and a smaller boy. They had come down to the beach from a trailer at the top of the bluff, only to be set upon by a wet and affectionate Airedale. He was lavishing saltwater kisses on their arms and legs.

"He won't hurt you," I assured the children, panting up to their rescue. "He just likes people."

I collared the dog and tugged him away and we headed back down the beach. The dog peeled off, chasing sea gulls in the surf, and was far behind when I reached the gully. There was no sign of the swimmers in the water. I looked toward their camp and saw them sunning facedown on the blanket, oblivious of my approach. For a moment I thought the two girls were wearing bikinis of palest pink. They looked warm and nubile and voluptuous. Then, as I drew closer, the surf drowning out the crunch of my tennis shoes in the pebbles, I realized they weren't wearing anything at all.

I stood still, wondering what to do. What did good

breeding require? It occurred to me that I should simply walk quietly on, but if I passed them to climb back up the ramp they would see me and know I had seen them. I rather thought they wouldn't mind; but I did.

Then, with horror, I remembered the Airedale. He was bounding toward us, only seconds away, his muzzle dripping seaweed; bounding toward our little quartet, only one of whom had any idea what was about to happen —that one being me. In a moment he would discover the delectable prizes on the blanket and strike, I had no doubt, like a bomber, delivering frigid kisses to whatever targets a bountiful fate provided.

The prospect was utterly absorbing. I could hardly move. I ached to witness the impending action. My eye fluttered between the closing Airedale and his prey, so pink and vulnerable and unsuspecting. But then, in a lucid flash, I foresaw that in the midst of the excitement which surely must ensue, my own presence would be discovered. I would somehow be identified as the villain-provocateur of the episode, and I would not likely get out of it by saying, "He won't hurt you—he just likes people."

Not a split second too soon I turned and ran toward the surf and the Airedale saw me and veered off his disastrous course, never to know what he had missed. We ran on down the beach and made a difficult climb up the rocks to the house.

We had acted with prudence; and I, for one, will always regret it.

When we leave Bocana to drive back to Los Angeles—a journey which under ideal nonstop circumstances takes five hours—I always add half an hour to our estimated

time of arrival to cover the unexpected. That weekend the
Airedale provided the unexpected. Sunday afternoon,
when the car was packed and we were ready to leave, he
could not be found.

"He was here five minutes ago," Denny said.

I looked out over the landscape into which he had
vanished. If he was out there somewhere, he was invisible
against the protective coloration of earth and flora. I
strained my eyes for any sign of movement.

Sea gulls were circling the spot where we had set out
our fruit and watermelon rind, circling and landing, taking off and circling and landing, like student pilots. A
hawk was stunting in the sky, working alone. A man and
a woman and a boy were down on the pebble beach. The
tide was out and they were riding motorcycles back and
forth on the flat sand below the pebbles. In the distance
the motorcycles sounded like hornets on a summer day.

"He's taken up with someone," I said, "and followed
them off."

We waited and called and whistled, but I knew he had
gone beyond the limits of his previous sorties.

"You suppose he's lost?"

"No. Dogs don't get lost in this kind of country. He's
having a good time somewhere, damn him."

We drove toward Bocana. Halfway there we met a boy
on a motorbike, coming our way. I stopped and shouted
at him.

"Did you see an Airedale anywhere?"

He thought. "What's an Airedale?"

"It's a big red dog," I said.

"Not red," Denny said. "Mostly black, on top, anyway,
and kind of bronzy."

"Big shaggy dog," I said.

"No, not shaggy. I'd say more raggedy."

The boy shook his head. He was eager to be on his way.

We drove on to Bocana. The dog hadn't been there. There was news, though. Lisa, the Gomez bitch, had whelped. I wondered if the Airedale would sire the next litter. Not if I could help it.

We drove back over the road and past the house and headed for the port, seeing no sign of man or dog until we got there. A young man, an American, was standing outside the weather-beaten store with a can of beer in his hand.

"Have you seen an Airedale over here?" I called out.

"An Airedale," he said. "What does an Airedale look like? Exactly."

"Kind of a big dog," I said. "Sort of a reddish bronze color. Mostly black on top. Not shaggy so much as raggedy, if you know what I mean."

He nodded as the description struck home. "Yes. There was a dog like that around here. Just a few minutes ago."

"Was he with another dog?"

"He was with some people. A man and his wife and some kids. Out hiking. Come to think of it, they had a dog, too."

I saw some boys with two dogs playing at the end of the point, where the sea sprays over the rocks. I walked out and asked them if they'd seen an Airedale, giving the description.

"What's his name?" one of the boys asked.

"Pugsley. Fleetwood Pugsley."

He shook his head. "No dog named that around here."

We caught up with him on the road back. He was with

a man and woman with three children and a black dog. One big happy family.

"Here Pugs!" we called. "Here Fleetwood!"

He bounded up to the car and leaped in. The man walked over.

"What's the name you're calling him?" he asked.

"Fleetwood Pugsley," I said.

"Well," he said, "we call him Jake."

I added one hour to our ETA.

CHAPTER FOURTEEN

That winter, as the work drew near to an end, we made few trips to Bocana. The men would be working inside, finishing the cabinets and setting the tile. It would be cold in the house and the road would be muddy from the rains.

One Thursday night in February, though, I drove down to spend a long Washington's Birthday weekend. I loaded the car in a hurry, wanting to reach the house by midnight. My wife was staying home, so I took the Airedale for company.

"I'll pack the cool can for you," she said. "Will a half-gallon of milk be enough?"

It sounded like plenty. There is something to be said for the division of domestic responsibilities by sex, however much the feminists appear to resent it as a male chauvinist arrangement. She always packed the cool can, while I attended to the firewood and the needs of the car. Switching these traditional roles might well result in an unstable marriage, or at least a dreary weekend.

When I arrived Gomez's store was dark. I drove on past it and along the bluffs past the Millard house and Luczynski house, and the Schmidt site, and finally I was home.

I opened the front door to go in and then it struck me

that I had never opened the front door before. We had never had a front door. I examined it by flashlight. It was a fine heavy door, made of 1 1/2-inch planks, with reinforcing crossbeams bolted on. It was simple and handsome and strong, and it seemed exactly what I would have expected to come from Gomez's own hand. I was delighted at my wisdom in rejecting the $190 Guadalajara door. On this one point, at least, I had prevailed over Gomez.

I unloaded the car and opened the cool can to have a cold cup of milk. Cold milk is a ritual when we pull in late at night after the long drive. It soothes and refreshes and sustains. There was no milk. She had forgotten to pack the milk.

I was annoyed; immoderately annoyed, and annoyed with myself for being annoyed. Was I that hooked on milk? Was I a man or a boy? I could damn well get by for three days without my milk. All the same, I was annoyed.

I looked in the bar Salvador had built for us and found two bottles of Baja red wine I had left unopened. What providence!

I opened a bottle and had a cup of wine. It wasn't bad, and it seemed perfectly right to be drinking the local wine. It was Santo Tomás wine, and the grapes had very probably come from our valley, perhaps from vineyards first planted by the padres. "To the new door," I said, and had a second cup.

The next day, when I would ordinarily have drunk some milk with my lunch, I had some more of the wine instead. In the evening I finished the first bottle with dinner. Later I was reading by my Coleman lantern and thinking of opening the second bottle, for a nightcap, when I saw headlights. It was Luczynski's van. They had come down, as they often did, on Friday night after the workday.

Five minutes later someone came walking over the road toward our house with a lantern. It was Mrs. Luczynski. "This is from your wife," she said. She handed me a half-gallon carton of milk.

Denny had telephoned the Luczynskis in Los Angeles that morning and asked if they were driving to Baja for the weekend, and if so, would they mind picking up half a gallon of milk for me.

"She said to tell you it was with her love and apologies," said Mrs. Luczynski.

It had been good thinking on Denny's part, and touching. She had gone to some trouble, and so had the Luczynskis. I put the milk in the cool can and opened the second bottle of Baja red and drank a toast to all three of them.

In the morning I saw Gomez heading toward the house in his pickup. Something seemed slightly different about his approach, and in a moment I realized that one of his dogs was missing. I went outside to meet him.

"*Buenos días,*" I said. "You only have three dogs?"

"Firpo is gone," said Gomez. "He was very old and he was sick. I gave him poison."

The bluntness of it stunned me. It was the usual way of Gomez to couch the harsh realities of life in euphemism.

"You poisoned him?" I said. "Isn't that painful?"

"No, no, it is not painful," he said, his tone reproaching me for having such a thought. "I buy this little pill in Ensenada. I give Firpo a nice dinner. And then, in a little while, he is dead." He snapped a finger. "Like that. He does not suffer."

It should not, after all, have surprised me. Like God, Gomez did what he had to do.

The Airedale was in the house, looking out the window at Gomez's dogs. He was excited but silent, evidently so moved he was voiceless. I opened the door for Gomez and he entered, but his dogs declined. They are half-wild and will not enter a house, even when the door is left open. They stayed on the porch, looking in the windows with their lupine eyes.

"Romulo," I said, "the door is beautiful."

"Of course," he said. "I made the door myself."

"It couldn't be better."

"Gracias, señor."

"How much will it cost?" I knew it was crass to intrude on a moment of aesthetic appreciation with a question of money, but I was feeling vindicated about the door, and was eager to know how much I had saved.

"Don't worry about the cost, Jack," said Gomez.

"I have to worry about the cost. There's a limit."

"I wish you owed me a million dollars."

I gave up on the door and turned to the local news. I asked about the new roads. Gossip had reached me in Los Angeles. One was being built by some mysterious developer, up and over the hill behind the port, and the other was being built by some mysterious competitor, around the hill on the far side. Both, it was said, were heading for a piece of coastal land to which each claimed title.

"Those birds," said Gomez, using an Americanism he used only to express disdain, "they do not have the title, neither one."

"We are lucky," I said, "that only Romulo Gomez has the title to *this* land."

Gomez smiled sadly. He has a pliant and patrician face,

much like the face, I should imagine, of a Roman senator; and when his honor is in the least impugned his smile reflects a disarming sadness. His eyes harden and soften almost at once, and as soon as you are reproached, you are forgiven.

After Gomez left, the Airedale went to the window again, his ears up, and again he was silent. It was Pablo the fisherman. I was annoyed with the dog. Pablo is a formidable looking stranger of the kind a watchdog ought to bark at.

He had brought a sack full of cod, fresh caught. His boots were still wet. The fish was pink and glistening. It would make a tasty dinner, but then I would be wasting the pound of hamburger my wife had packed.

I bought three filets from Pablo and cooked them that evening over a low flame, the way Gomez had taught me, turning them just as they started to brown. I ate them with nothing but a little salt and the last of the wine. It was a feast, and it left me for a moment euphoric. The dog got the pound of hamburger and the rest of the milk, and I knew why he hadn't barked at Pablo, the bringer of gifts.

If my talks with Gomez sometimes left me less than serene, I was again heartened by the thought that our new neighbor, Hal Schmidt, was not some financial illiterate like me, but a man who had achieved high office in the corporate world. Here was a neighbor whose very presence would quiet our doubts. As his house arose, every brick would be a new testament to our own security.

It was the next evening that I finally met the Schmidts for the first time. He and his wife were staying for the weekend with the Millards, and the Millards had invited

me over for cocktails. Recently Gordon and Opal Millard
had sold their house in Pasadena and moved to Baja. As
American citizens, they would be required to renew their
visitors' permits every six months, but they now regarded
Baja as their home. Their two daughters were grown.
Millard had taken early retirement; he was in his late
fifties, I imagined, with graying hair and a craggy face. He
was lean, tanned and hardened by his long solitary walks
over the Baja hills. He was a taciturn man; his voice was
soft and his words gentle. The Millards had adapted
wholeheartedly to the rustic life. They were learning to
speak Spanish, and had made friends with Abel and other
residents of the valley, where they obtained the red chiles
and green peppers and tomatoes and squashes that had
become a mainstay of their kitchen.

Millard had built a tool and generator house and
bought a small generator, so they had electric lights. But
they were small and few, and candlelight still gave their
living room its charm, flickering on the brick walls and in
the arched recesses and over Millard's paintings.

There was a portrait of one of the girls who lived in the
valley and sometimes helped Delia Gomez in the kitchen.
She was a beautiful girl, at the threshold of womanhood,
and Millard had done her well. He had wanted to paint her
ever since he first saw her, he said, but she had been too
shy.

"It turned out she had heard all about us artists, and
thought I wanted to paint her in the nude. Then one day
she came with a friend, a chaperone, of course, and
posed."

Millard poured Santo Tomás wine and it was in the
warmth of his house that I had my first talk with Schmidt.
He looked in his forties, and his wife younger. They were

a handsome couple. Schmidt talked easily and well; you knew he was an efficient and exacting man, but there was a touch of the romantic that surprised and pleased me.

Right at the outset, he said, he had very nearly brought disaster on his house. He had drawn the plans himself, as I had ours. His wife had then redrawn them to scale, but in feet and inches, of course, and, as required by the Mexican law, they had to be redrawn by a Mexican architect, to change them into the metric system and to make sure that all was according to the Mexican building code.

"The Mexican architect made no changes," Schmidt said. "We were rather proud of that. It was an implication that our planning had been sound. But he *added* just one thing."

"What was that?" I asked.

"Our living room, you know, is fifty feet wide. The Mexican architect added an enormous pillar in the very center of the room, without which, we found out, the entire house would have collapsed."

"All the same," I said, "I'm certainly glad to have you with us."

"Oh?" he said.

"Yes. When I heard who you were in the financial world," I explained, "I knew you would do all the things I ought to have done and didn't. Hire a lawyer. Search the title. Study the economic factor. Find out exactly where we stand."

"Why, no," said Schmidt. "I assumed *you* would have done all that. I haven't done a thing. I don't have anything but one of those open-end contracts. My faith is in Gomez."

Suddenly both of us laughed. We were like the boy in

the story Jack Kennedy used to tell. When he came to a high wall and was afraid to climb it to see what was on the other side he threw his hat over, and then he had to go after his hat. Schmidt and I had thrown our hats.

Late in April Gomez telephoned us from Tijuana.

"*Señor,*" he said, "your house is finished."

Here it was at last, the unimaginable culmination, the dream fulfilled; and I was unable to think of anything but trivial details.

"Everything is done?" I said. "You've cleaned up all the debris?"

"Everything," said Gomez. "It is clean like a whistle."

I felt uneasy. Sometimes when Gomez uses the American idiom it is harder to appraise his meaning than when he withdraws into Spanish.

"The toilet," I said. "It is in?"

"*Sí, señor.*"

Doubts formed like a cloud. I had learned that when Gomez said "*Sí, señor,*" he was not necessarily answering in the affirmative, but sometimes merely acknowledging the viability of one's question.

We couldn't get away until Friday night, and then we stopped in Ensenada, not wanting to push on at so late an hour. It would be better, we agreed, to see the finished house for the first time in the daylight.

All misgivings evaporated Saturday morning as we drove south in the warm spring morning, through Maneadero, which was coming awake for a big weekend, and over the hills into the valley. For once I drove the dirt road without mishap, and we emerged at the mouth of the river with pulses rising. Gomez was not in his store.

"Oh, he's over at your house," said Mrs. Gomez, "finishing up. He got up at six o'clock."

Finishing up? I wondered what that meant. We drove up the hill and came to the point from which we could see the house standing out on the bluff. I stopped the car and we let our eyes devour it: the house, the rocky coves, the earth, the crescent beach, the sea, the sky.

Denny sighed. "Oh, Lord," she said, "it's beautiful." Gomez's pickup was parked outside. His dogs surrounded us. Inside the house a radio was playing *"La Golondrina."* We heard men's voices. We opened the beautiful front door and looked tentatively into our living room. The interior too was beautiful, with the vaulted ceiling and wood beams, the red tile floor, the brick walls, and the brilliant tiles around the sink and on the bartop.

And squarely in the center of the room, stark and shocking, was a toilet.

Gomez came out of the bathroom. *"Buenos días,"* he said grandly.

"Buenos días," I said. "The toilet is not in?"

Gomez explained. There had been some last minute problem with the plumbing. It was nothing. In half an hour our toilet would be installed in the bathroom and working like a whistle.

We were strangely unperturbed. It didn't seem to matter. Denny paid hardly any attention to Gomez's explanation. She stood just inside the doorway, transfixed by what she saw; her eyes were moist as they caressed the colors and lines and textures of her living room.

The toilet was yellow, as we had wanted it to be, and it looked brand new. There was also a yellow range in place, and a yellow gas refrigerator. Both were obviously of an ancient vintage. But that they were here at all was remarkable. The range apparently had been yellow from the start; the refrigerator had been freshly painted. Gomez had gone to a lot of trouble to satisfy our taste.

Denny threw her arms around Gomez and kissed him on the cheek. "Romulo," she said, "it's wonderful."

"You have a mansion," said Gomez.

He excused himself and went back into the bathroom, from which there then came the sound of low voices and the clink of pipes and wrenches. Besides Gomez in the room, I saw, were the tile man, the carpenter, and a boy, Alberto, Pablo the fisherman's son.

They all greeted us warmly and we left them to their work and went out to sit on the front porch, brimming with a sweet sense of possessing and being possessed. Two strangers from Los Angeles came by to compliment us on our fortune in owning such a house, and as we talked with them on the porch Gomez at last appeared.

"It is finished," he said. "I am going to make it work. You wish to see?"

We crowded into the bathroom—my wife and I and the strangers from Los Angeles and Gomez and his workers and the boy. The toilet was in place. Gomez stood beside it. With an air of ceremony, he reached out a finger and depressed the chromium lever. There was an overture of rushing water, then a rippling scherzo, a gurgling Wagnerian climax—and finally a sweet triumphant silence.

We could have wept.

CHAPTER FIFTEEN

The house was splendid. Gomez had triumphed. In every detail, in the set of the brick, the grace of the arches, the heft and thrust of the open beams, it was, as Gomez had always said it would be, a mansion.

Inevitably, though, like any new house, it had its peculiar imperfections; some our fault, some perhaps the fault of Gomez, and some of God. They soon began to reveal themselves. For one thing, the tile in the kitchen was blue. As I remembered it, Gomez had suggested blue tile that day in Tijuana, but we had picked green. Oh well, the blue was pretty enough.

I personally discovered that the toilet, which had worked so beautifully in its premiere engagement, seemed to be connected to the hot water. In all my experience with plumbing, the world over, I had never encountered this astonishing eccentricity.

That first evening, when Denny began to wash the dishes, she discovered yet another hydrothermal quirk. "They've got the water backwards in the sink," she said.

"What do you mean backwards?"

"The hot water faucet runs cold and the cold runs hot."

That evening after sundown a chill wind came up from

the sea, and it occurred to me that we had yet to try our fireplace. I had never lived in a house with a fireplace, and the prospect of a crackling fire on a windy night had been one of the joys I most looked forward to in the Baja house.

Pablo had brought us some oak logs from the valley, and with a sense of long-delayed fulfillment I began to build our fire. I knew I was no expert at building fires, but soon I had one going. Tongues of flame reached up, throwing a wild and sinuous light on the dark brick walls. Waves of heat flowed out and enveloped us, and we were content.

Then I saw a wisp of smoke escape. It was soon followed by a puff, and then a cloud, and in a minute smoke was billowing into the room. Crying and choking we ran to open the doors and windows to the cold sea wind. When the room cleared, I rebuilt the fire, and for a while it behaved, but as soon as the kindling flames burned down, the smoke came. Again and again I tried, each time with the same discouraging results.

We went outside and shone a flashlight up to the top of the chimney. There was a little cupola over the chimney, with a tile roof. It was open on two sides, and now and then a puff of smoke would come out. Then a gust of wind would come up from the sea and blow the smoke back into the cupola and down the chimney.

"You know what I think?" Denny said. "If you would make that little cupola up there open on all four sides, and raise it to make the openings bigger, then the wind would blow through it and the smoke would blow away."

"I'm afraid," I said, "it isn't that simple."

At last I put the fire out and threw water on the embers. We put on sweaters and sat in our Thrifty Drug Store chairs. I stared at the fireplace with a kind of hate.

In the entire enterprise, this was the darkest moment I had known. The fireplace was an integral part of a house, stone of its stone. I remembered some folklore. When a fireplace was made wrong, it could never be made right. Our fireplace was the core, the heart, of our house; and it was wrong. We were ruined.

In the morning the sun came over the hill and into the kitchen and we didn't need the fireplace. Denny made coffee and opened the refrigerator to get things out for breakfast.

"That's funny," she said. "The milk's frozen."

"The milk's frozen?"

"Come and look."

Not only the milk was frozen; the meat we had brought down in the cool can was frozen; the lettuce was frozen; the eggs were frozen.

"Frozen eggs," she said, "I have never seen."

"It must be set too high," I said. "I'll check the thermostat."

But the thermostat was set at "Least Cold," only one stop away from "Defrost." I had a sinking feeling, a premonition that there was something essentially and perhaps fatally wrong with our newly painted yellow refrigerator.

We were glad to see Gomez heading toward the house.

"*Buenos días,*" he said. "Is everything all right in your mansion this morning?"

I told him about the hot water in the toilet. "I guess it's harmless," I said, "but it *is* quite unusual."

He laughed. "I will explain that, Jack."

He had laid several hundred feet of plastic pipe down

the hill to our house from the reservoir, and he had left the trench temporarily unfilled, so that if any leaks developed he could find them.

"So the sun," he said, "in the daytime she shines on your pipe and makes your water hot, you see?"

"I see. We've got solar heating in the toilet. Fantastic."

Denny told him about the faucets over the sink.

"Don't worry," Gomez said. "I will take care of that."

He went out to the truck and came back with some wrenches. We busied ourselves elsewhere while Gomez worked at the sink. He was finished in five minutes.

"It's okay now," he said. "You try it."

Denny turned on the faucet to her left and held a hand under the stream. "It's still cold," she said.

"Of course," said Gomez. "It is cold. You see?"

He pointed to the letters on the handles. The C for "cold" was on the left. He had simply reversed the handles.

I told him about the refrigerator. "It's freezing everything," I said. "Look." I opened the door and took out a dish of olives that had a crust of ice.

Gomez got down on his knees to check the thermostat. "It is on 'Least Cold,' " he said.

"Yes. That's the warmest setting."

He turned the dial carefully and stood up. "Now it will be all right," he said. "I have put it on 'Medium.' "

"But Romulo," I said, "that will make it even worse. 'Medium' is colder than 'Least Cold.' "

"Not in Baja," said Gomez.

"Maybe we'd better tell him about the fireplace," Denny said.

"Yes. The fireplace smokes."

"It cannot smoke," said Gomez. "It is American."

He explained that the fireplace was built around a Heatilator, American-made, and so it could not fail.

"All right," I said. "Let's see you try it."

"Of course," he said. He built a small fire and stood back, watching as the flames took hold. The fire was blameless, the smoke and flame vanishing up the flue.

"You see, *señor*," said Gomez. "It is all right."

He turned around to face me and at that moment a puff of smoke escaped.

"There," I said, "you see?"

He turned again. The smoke had dissipated on the fresh currents in the room.

"You missed it," I said. "As soon as you turned your back it smoked."

"What I think," Denny said, "is that if you opened that little house over the chimney on all four sides and made the openings bigger, the smoke would blow away."

"Don't worry," said Gomez, "it will not smoke any more."

It probably wouldn't, I thought. There was some kind of magic in Mr. Gomez.

"Did you notice," I said after Gomez left, "the damn thing didn't smoke until he turned his back?"

With a fireplace that smoked, a refrigerator that froze eggs, and a toilet that ran hot water, I could hardly consider the house finished. But I was eager to settle up with Gomez. I had no doubt that he would finish the job. I wanted to know where we stood. We had already paid much more than the amount of the original estimate, and by tacit agreement the piece of paper on which that figure was written had long since been abrogated. It was no longer realistic. Prices had soared; the dimensions of the house had expanded; there had been many extras, some of them our own ideas, some Gomez's.

It was true also that we had left it to Gomez to supply the refrigerator, range, toilet, and kitchen sink, which originally were to have been supplied by the owner. Some of them, I imagined, had been foraged at the expenditure of much energy and wile, as well as money.·

That Sunday afternoon he came by with a smudged and tattered envelope. It was our file. It contained a sheaf of bills he had paid on our behalf, and a long column of figures written in pencil on a ragged-edged sheet of lined schoolroom paper. At the bottom was the amount due, and the total.

"Well," I said, "it isn't as bad as I thought. It's hardly more than twice as much as my absolute top figure."

"I don't care," Denny said.

I didn't care either. It would have cost at least twice as much again to build a house such as this in Los Angeles; very likely three times as much; and it would never have been as good. We seem no longer to have the craftsmen in the United States, nor the integrity.

"And your beautiful door," said Gomez, "you are satisfied?"

I looked down the list of items until I found it:

Main door—Handmade by R. Gomez . . . $90.00

Ninety dollars for a door handmade by R. Gomez was a lot more than $20 for a door by Sears Roebuck; but it was also a lot less than $190 for a door from Guadalajara.

"Romulo," I said, "the door is a great bargain. *Gracias.*"

The amount due was $4,755.76. I told him we would send him a check as soon as we could gather the money. "There is no hurry, Jack," he said. "I wish you owed me a million dollars."

The next time we went to Bocana we took our neighbors the Daltons. They were our first house guests, and we hoped everything would go well.

The road had dried after the spring rains and had been graded again. There was no incident to upset anyone, except for the snake we ran over.

"Was he a rattlesnake?" asked Sara Dalton.

"It doesn't matter," I said. "He was dead."

All the same, I knew it was a rattler, and it made me uneasy. Gomez had said we would never find a rattlesnake at our house because they wouldn't cross his road. But it was not a particularly credible bit of folklore. The Baja peninsula was notoriously hospitable to rattlesnakes, and a dead one in the valley was a closer thing than I cared for.

When we reached Bocana we stopped at the store to report in and to get the local news.

"We saw a rattlesnake in the road coming in," I told Gomez as soon as the greetings were over.

"Oh, yes, there are snakes in the valley," he said.

I told him of hearing that Millard had killed two rattlers outside his house so far that spring.

"Oh, yes," he said. "Mrs. Millard, she waters her plants too much. The little snakes, they come for the water."

"But you said they would never cross the road."

"Of course they do not cross the road, but they will cross the road if they are thirsty."

Our house looked shipshape, but we hardly had the car unloaded before Denny cried out in dismay. "We've had a mouse!" She was bent over the Luczynski chair, looking at something.

"How do you know?" I asked.

"Here's its spoor."

It was a revelation to me. I had no idea she even knew the word "spoor." Spoor has a primitive aura. It evokes man's earliest hour on earth, when he hunted and was hunted, each species sniffing at the other's traces.

"Let's have a look," said Dalton, peering down at the Luczynski chair. "Uh huh. I think the word you want is stool, not spoor."

"Well, whatever," Denny said. "It's a mouse."

I thought no more about it until I got my pajamas out of the closet that night. There was a network of holes in the shoulder and another in the chest.

"What could have done this?" I asked. "Dry rot?"

"That's your mouse," said Dalton.

"Why would he eat my pajamas? Pajamas aren't nourishing, are they?"

"They eat paper," Denny said.

I was impressed. She knew more about mice than I did. It only confirmed the feminists in their complaint that woman's intellectual reach is limited by her imprisonment in the home. Let her out in the jungle and what she knows about the house mouse she would soon enough know about the mamba and the crocodile.

"Actually," Dalton said, "it's the cellulose."

The next morning the mouse appeared in person. I was sitting in the Luczynski chair, having a cup of coffee with Dalton while the women were washing the breakfast dishes. It was Dalton who saw him first.

"Don't move," he said, "your mouse is out."

"Out? Out where?"

"Too late. He ran out from under that chair you're sitting in, and then he ran back."

"Good God," I said, leaping up. I shoved the chair aside but the mouse was gone.

"I shouldn't be surprised," Dalton said, "if the little beggar weren't living in that chair."

Dalton had fallen into one of his double negatives, but it was no time to cavil about grammar.

"Let's just turn it over," he said, "and have a look."

We turned the chair over on its side. The cloth bottom had been holed. Just as I bent down for a closer look the mouse popped out. He was hardly more than a gray movement, so tiny and fleeting I thought it might have been a moth. Then it darted across the red tile floor and stopped in front of the open outside door.

"Out!" I shouted at him. "Get out! Hear?"

It sometimes works with dogs and cats, but apparently not with mice. He missed his chance. He ran back across the floor and into the back bedroom. I got the mop from the porch and a cardboard carton.

"Here," I said to Denny, "you hold the box and I'll chase him into it with the mop. I'm going to get him alive and give him back to Luczynski."

"Are you kidding?" she said. "I'm washing the dishes."

I finished my coffee first, planning my tactics. Then I went into the bedroom with the mop and the box and shut the door. I was alone in there with the mouse, and only one of us came out alive.

I took the carcass out in the box and threw it into the cactus where the scavengers would find it and went back into the house with the mop over my shoulder. The women didn't look up from their dishes. One plays one's role in life.

I thought of moving the Luczynski chair out on the porch. If it harbored one mouse, it very likely harbored more. Luczynski had given us a Trojan Horse. But I couldn't get rid of it yet. It was the only easy chair we had.

In midmorning we left the house to go down to the driftwood beach.

"Wait," Denny said, "I'd better get my purse."

"Never mind your purse," I said. "Those rocks and cliffs are too treacherous. You want to break a leg? You need your hands free."

"I think I'll just take a beer along," said Dalton.

We walked over the cliff to a point south of the driftwood beach where a descent is possible, if not easy. Like goats we picked our way down the rough lava seacliff, taking care with each step, always finding a handhold before moving on. I led the way, keeping an eye on Dalton. He had gone back for a bottle of Dos Equis, which is a rather heavy Mexican beer, but he kept his poise by moving it skillfully from hand to hand. Besides being a bird watcher, Dalton is something of an alpinist.

We all made it safely down to the beach. The women began gathering seashells. I leaped out over the tidepools and found a perch above the surf. What was it, I wondered, that made women gather seashells? It must go back to the shell cultures of primitive times. Before long Denny and Sara had their pockets bulging with shells, and we started up the cliff.

"Go ahead," Dalton said, "I'll just finish my beer."

We had been back at the house half an hour and were beginning to worry about Dalton when he appeared in the doorway. He was pale as a gaffed halibut. Blood streamed down his cheek from a cut above one eye. His left arm and leg were skinned.

"My God!" cried his wife.

Dalton walked unsteadily into the house. He put me in mind of Frankenstein's monster. He sank into a chair.

"Does anyone have a bandage?" he said.

"All we've got is Band-Aids," Denny said. "We'd better drive him in to the doctor."

"How many stitches do you think it would take?" I asked.

"At least one."

"There's no use driving forty miles for one stitch," I said. "Let's try the Band-Aid."

"I think I'd like a beer," said Dalton.

I opened a beer for him while Sara Dalton applied the Band-Aid. "You poor darling," she said.

I asked him what had happened. He took a swig of beer. "I was carrying the empty beer bottle in one hand. Didn't want to be a litterbug. Reached out to grab this big rock and the damn thing came loose. Hit me right in the eye."

"You mean you hit yourself in the eye with a rock?"

"In effect, yes. Then, of course, I fell."

"Let it be a lesson," I told my wife. "Get a first aid kit. It might have been me."

In the afternoon Denny went out to water the oleanders and we heard her cry out in dismay.

"It must be a snake," I said, running for the door.

"My God!" cried Sara Dalton.

"What is it?" I shouted, running up the bank to where she stood with the running water hose in her hand.

"Something's got two of my oleanders," she said.

The landscape was burgeoning. It was a gaudy spring. The mescals were near bursting with juices, their great flowers already out or swelling up inside their wraps. The mesembryanthemum my wife had planted on the bank in front of the house had unfurled a banner of purple. In this vernal affluence we had not noticed that two of our oleanders were missing. They simply weren't there, in their proper places.

"What do you suppose got them?" she asked, as if speaking of lambs that had been carried off by wolves.

"Gophers, most likely," Dalton said.

"Oleanders are poison," she said.

"Well, then," I pointed out, "all the more reason to hope the gophers got them."

She stood there, looking down at the evidence. "They've simply been nipped off," she said, "at the ground. Now what kind of an animal would do that?"

"Your oleander," Dalton said, "is probably not indigenous here."

"What's that got to do with it?" I asked.

"They wouldn't have a reputation among your local fauna for being poisonous," he said, "and my guess is that they've been sampled by some coyote, or maybe an iguana. Someone always has to go first in nature, I should think, to find out if things are edible."

We might never have known what had happened if we hadn't stopped at the store on the way home to say good-bye to Gomez.

I told him it had been fine except for the mouse and

the fact that we couldn't use the fireplace because of the smoke and the refrigerator froze the milk and eggs again.

"The man who cleaned up your yard," Gomez said, passing gracefully over my complaints. "He did a good job?"

"The man who cleaned the yard?"

"Yes, of course," said Gomez. "I told him to cut the weeds, in your garden." He made a motion like a man chopping with a machete. "Zick-zick," he said.

"Zick-zick," my wife said. Enlightenment came to her eyes.

"Yes, Romulo," she said, "he did a good job. Zick-zick."

"There's one good thing about it," Dalton said later, as we lurched back over the road. "If it was a man that got the oleanders, then it means you probably don't have an iguana."

Not having an iguana was the best thing that happened to us that weekend.

CHAPTER SIXTEEN

With the house finished, in a provisional sense, at least, we had to think of furniture. Our foldup cots and chairs had served us well enough in the construction period, but now we were impatient to furnish it in a style worthy of Gomez's workmanship. We wanted it to be Mexican, perhaps in the Spanish colonial tradition; handsome, sturdy, and comfortable as well.

The dining room set was to be the centerpiece of the house, the hub around which our domestic and social life would turn. It would set the tone. I could picture us at our table in the evenings, with the sun down in the bay and the fire burning in the fireplace, my wife at one end of the table like a duchess and myself at the other, telling our guests some charming anecdote by candlelight as we sipped the local wine.

We couldn't find anything in Ensenada to fit this picture. All the furniture in the local stores looked more like Grand Rapids than Guadalajara. Northern Baja was a young state, ambitious and aggressive, as the young states of the American west had been. Its people did not look back to colonial times; they were of today. They wanted plastics and transistors and Fords, just like their neighbors north of the border.

We had heard of Mexican colonial furniture stores in

Tijuana, but we could never get time enough in Tijuana to look; we were jealous of our days and always eager to push on to Bocana. Then one day I had a piece of luck. I saw an ad in the paper for a Los Angeles store that sold custom handmade Mexican furniture. It showed a dining room set of exactly the kind we wanted. The table was of the Durango style, mahogany, with carved scroll legs and a top two inches thick. The chairs were tall and sturdy looking, with seats and backs of genuine cowhide straps.

We drove out to the store and saw the set on the floor and were sold. It was twice as much as we had expected to pay; but it was like the arch in our house: the demands of artistic integrity gave us no choice. It must be ours.

I told the salesman we would like to have the set, but the problem then was how to get it across the border. If we could get it to Tijuana, Gomez could take it on down to Bocana in his truck. Did the salesman have any suggestions?

As it turned out, he couldn't have been more helpful. By the most fortunate coincidence, the store's factory was in Tijuana.

"I think it can be arranged," he said, "for you to pick up your set down there."

But the set on the floor was the only one in supply at the moment. An order would have to be put in at the factory for its duplication. It would take approximately a month. We paid for the set and waited. It was five weeks before a card came in the mail. Our furniture was now ready for delivery at the factory in Tijuana.

I phoned Gomez and arranged to meet him at the factory. I wanted to be sure we got the set we had asked for, and to see it safely onto Romulo's truck.

Gomez was happy to be of assistance, but I could see that something about the transaction troubled him.

"What is it, Romulo?" I asked, as we loaded the beautiful chairs.

"You bought this furniture in Los Angeles, Jack?"

"Yes. We were very lucky."

"You have paid the full price up there?"

"Yes, of course. They won't bargain with you in a Los Angeles furniture store."

"Then you have paid the duty, too, for bringing it into the United States?"

"Why, yes. I suppose the duty was included in the price."

He shook his head in gentle reproach. "You see, Jack, you have paid the duty to take your furniture into the United States, but your furniture, it has never left Mexico."

"But Romulo," I said, "if I had taken the set in Los Angeles, I would have had to take it across the border into Mexico. Isn't there some problem about taking American manufactured goods across the border?"

"But your furniture," he said, "it is made in Mexico."

The argument was growing attenuated; the logic was too fine a thread for me to follow.

"Also," said Gomez, "you have paid the cost of transporting your furniture from Tijuana to Los Angeles."

"But isn't that offset," I said, trying one last gambit, "by not having to transport it from Los Angeles to Tijuana?"

"It would have cost you less," Gomez said, "to bring the furniture from Guadalajara on the train. The furniture of Guadalajara is the most beautiful furniture of Mexico."

We did buy new beds in Ensenada though, and had a chair and settee custom-made for us in the Spanish colonial style, and one day, after we had found the mouse nest in the Luczynski chair, I drove into town to look for a new recliner to read in. I could not go on sitting in the Luczynski chair. I had found no way to correct its tilt to the left, so I had been obliged either to keep my head tilted to the right, or hold my book crooked. I was afraid I would become permanently askew.

Going to town is a festive occasion down in Baja, as it used to be in rural America. It is forty-five miles to Ensenada, and at that time the road was even more unpredictable than usual. They were widening the paved road and it was trapped with dusty detours, not to mention slow-moving vehicles, dogs, chickens and pedestrians and, occasionally, a loaded burro, and a checkpoint had been set up where soldiers looked in your car, for smuggled guns and drugs, we imagined.

Ever since Denny had punctured the gas tank on her car, we were taking the dirt road slower than we used to. It had taken several blown tires, a set of shock absorbers, two cracked transmission cases and then the ruptured gas tank to make us see the wisdom of slowing down and enjoying the landscape, instead of fighting it.

We had driven down in my old Dodge convertible, and with the top down I felt more a part of the valley than ever before as I headed for Ensenada over the dirt road past the communal farms and their adobe houses. Children waved. The women could be seen looking out from the dark interiors of the adobes through open doors or bending over their iron washtubs in the yard. The men were out in the fields plowing or harvesting, some with horses and some with tractors. Two dogs chased me half a mile, yipping along by my wheels, out of sight. Even the cows and horses turned to give me a look and I had plenty of time to adjust to the sudden rabbit or squirrel in the road without blowing a tire on a rock.

In Ensenada I went to the *supermercado*. It is very much like a Los Angeles supermarket, except that the prices are in pesos and the checkers calculate your bill in dollars, sometimes doing it with a pencil on the tape, more often in their heads. I bought three quarts of milk, a case of beer, a sack of dog food and a package of tortillas, and then went into the furniture store next door to look for the easy chair.

There were only two recliners in the store. They were both large and ungainly, made of foam rubber and vinyl. One was a sky blue and one a daisy yellow, but they were otherwise identical. They weren't what I had in mind.

"Do you have any more?" I asked the salesman. He was short and portly, with a solemn face and a spade beard that made him look more like an intellectual revolutionary than a furniture salesman.

"Come," he said, and he led me into a half-dark storage room behind the showroom. There among the crowded stock he found a third chair, exactly like the others but for its color, which was fuchsia.

"I think I prefer the yellow one," I said.

We went back into the showroom and I sat in the yellow chair, trying all its three positions. It was a bit too high in the air, and firmer than I had hoped; somewhat like a horse. But it was the only chair in the place, other than the sky blue and the fuchsia.

On the way back I got the chair through the checkpoint without incident, though the soldiers looked into my glove compartment and trunk and even my sack of groceries. I thought of Luczynski and how he had used his chair to smuggle his mice into our house, but I didn't say anything. A checkpoint is no place for jokes.

When I reached the house I found Denny sitting quite still in the living room. She looked unnerved.

"What was it this time?" I asked.

She told me the story, trying to make it sound casual, but there was a special tremor in her voice. Something had shaken her.

"For one thing," she said, "we have another mouse."

"How do you know?"

"I saw him. Several times."

Several times? Suddenly it struck me; what should have been obvious all along. She hadn't seen just one mouse several times. She had seen several mice at least once. The Luczynski mouse had been virile indeed, and now his progeny were taking possession of our mansion.

"Well," I said, "we aren't going to let a few mice drive us out."

"That isn't all."

"What else?"

"We had a rattlesnake."

My skin turned cold.

She had gone out on the little back porch and reached down to pick up a pony flat of daisies to plant and the snake crawled away from beside the flat.

"He wasn't six inches from my hand."

"What did you do?"

"I went in and took two aspirin and lay down."

"You didn't kill the snake?"

"Well, I had a kind of a headache, anyway, and I just thought that if I took some aspirin and lay down, maybe it would go away."

"You mean the headache?"

"I guess I hoped the snake would go away, too."

She had never encountered a rattlesnake before, except in a zoo. She didn't know how fast they could travel; how quick they could coil and strike. She didn't know whether she could kill one.

"I don't know whether I didn't have the courage," she said, "or the heart."

"You were scared?"

"Yes." She looked downcast. "I thought I was more of a pioneer than that."

She had lain down for a while and then got up and gone out to see if the snake was still there.

"He was over by the water heater. He had three rattles. He had a flat head and a forked tongue. He kept darting it out at me."

"What did you do?"

"I drove over to the store to get Romulo."

Gomez had not been at the store, but young Sergio got his shotgun and went over to the house in his pickup to kill the snake.

"He killed it?"

"It was gone."

Later Gomez had come by to ask about the snake.

"What did he say?"

"He said it was probably confused by the new road, and didn't know which side it was supposed to stay on."

So the snake was still alive. I imagined him breeding. Soon there would be a dozen more. It was an unsettling prospect, and one that a bit of resolution and clear thinking might easily have forestalled. I remembered how quickly and efficiently I had dealt with the mouse.

"If 'twere to be done," I told her, " 'twere best 'twere done quickly."

I wondered, though, how quickly it would have been done if I had been in her place.

When I had the yellow chair in the house I moved the Luczynski chair into the smaller bedroom, which was to be our guest room. Denny said that if the chair had mice, she'd rather it was in the guest room.

In the back of my mind, though, was a plan. When Gomez finished the house he was building for the Schmidts, I would give the chair to them, temporarily, as Luczynski had given it to us. One neighborly good turn deserves another.

The next weekend we headed for Mexico to deal with the rodents once and for all, without sentiment.

We left on Friday after work and it was dark when we reached the border. Just north of the international gate we had one of those irritating confrontations with a driver who was determined not to let us into a slow-moving line of traffic. We had pulled off the highway to gas up, and were trying to cut back in. My mood had been bad enough to start with, and the incident made me irrationally angry.

Traffic tends to be heavy at this point, especially on Friday night, as the lanes funnel into the gate, and no one likes to give up his position. I saw an opening, though, in front of a brand-new yellow Ford van. The driver was up high on the seat so I couldn't see him to give him a friendly supplicating look. I simply edged a fender in, hoping he would respect his own fender, if not mine. To my annoyance, he moved by me. I turned into the shoulder and drew up beside him. Again a gap appeared and I started to ease in. He closed the gap.

"Ugly damn American," I muttered.

"The woman in front of him is holding up," Denny said.

Indeed she was. A gap was widening ahead of her. I hit the gas and passed her and turned into the space ahead of her and moved on toward the border, ahead of the woman and the van. I laughed.

"What are you laughing at?"

"That s.o.b. in the yellow van. I bet I gave him apoplexy."

We popped through the bottleneck of the border and skirted Tijuana. The Ensenada freeway unrolled before us under the starlight. As we sped south I wondered why automobiles turned people into ogres. Behind the wheel, people suspended the ordinary rules of courtesy that made life agreeable in other social situations. They seemed to become integral parts of the machines they controlled. They were less than human. I was often snarled and cursed at by drivers who, if they were to meet me five minutes later in front of an elevator, would smile when the doors slid open, insisting with a nod and an upturned palm that I should by all means enter before them. Often enough I had also found myself shouting "Idiot!" at some idiot, only to realize with chagrin a moment later that he or perhaps she was probably a fairly decent fellow, like me, although not as good a driver.

We stopped in Ensenada for dinner and reached the house after midnight. Our neighbors' houses were dark, but the Luczynskis were down. We could see their van parked out front in the starlight.

We lighted a Coleman and my wife went into the bathroom and in a minute I heard a shriek. She came out of the bathroom holding her plastic shower cap.

"Look at this."

"What is it?"

"My shower cap. It's full of dog kibbles."

"How could that happen?"

"The mice."

We lighted another lantern and began our inspection. It was obvious the mice had got into the ten-pound sack of kibbled dog food I had brought down to the house for the Airedale. Holes had been gnawed in the sack and they had been removing the kibbles one by one and storing them in caches all over the house.

One cache was in a pretty enameled teapot Denny used as a flower holder. It was crammed with kibbles to the spout. There were kibbles in the drawer of the nightstand by the bed. There were kibbles in all seven drawers of the semainier. We had to admire their skill and industry. How had they ever reached that shower cap as it hung from the arm of a chromium towel tree in the bath?

At one time, I reflected sadly, we had hoped to compromise with the little beggars; live and let live. Give them their secret runs in the dark recesses of the cupboards. But they had a critical advantage over us. They occupied the ground permanently. We were only casual visitors. It was no contest. We were overrun.

Not only had we provided them with food enough to raise many generations, but with a scientifically balanced diet, as set forth on the sack: "Exceeds nutritional requirements for mature dogs established by the National Research Council and provides all the known vitamins and minerals needed for good health."

We were breeding supermice. With their notorious virility fortified by all the known minerals and vitamins, they would very likely proliferate like Huns and soon enough ride out from our house to overrun the entire peninsula of Baja California.

We spent an uneasy night and got up early to fight back.

That morning the Luczynskis walked over to see if they could help. No doubt Luczynski was feeling guilty about the chair.

"What you ought to do," he said, "is put out some rat poison."

"Rat poison!" The sound of it made me shudder.

"Works like a charm," he said. "You just set it out around your house in abalone shells, every ten feet or so, along the walls. In two weeks you won't have a mouse. They never come back."

I hated the idea of poison, but the time had come for counterattack. We must bow to the realities, not only for ourselves, but for the Republic of Mexico.

"If you want to walk over," Luczynski said, "I can let you have some. I've got an extra box."

Denny had been talking meanwhile with Mrs. Luczynski. She turned to me.

"Do you know who that was last night," she said, "in the yellow van? At the border?"

I started to say no, I didn't; and then of course it came to me.

"Luczynski!"

"Do you want to know," asked Mrs. Luczynski, "what he said about you?"

"No," I said, "I don't think I do."

"He said you were a hostile bastard."

"That's all right," I said. "I called him an ugly American s.o.b."

I walked back with Luczynski to his house, both of us laughing over the incident at the border. How ironic it was. He had called me a bastard and I had called him an s.o.b., and now he was going to share his poison with me.

"I'll build a fire," I said that evening, though not with much enthusiasm.

"Let's pray it doesn't smoke," my wife said.

The fireplace had never worked right yet, except when Gomez was in the house. The last time we had built a fire we had been driven out by smoke, coughing and weeping, and had gone to the store and confronted Gomez with the evidence of our reddened eyes and ashen faces. He had agreed that the problem of the fireplace must be reviewed.

Now, perversely, it seemed to be drawing smartly. There was a good roar and the flames rushed up toward the flue.

"He must have done something," I said.

I went outside and looked up at the chimney. The little roof over the top of the flue had been opened up on all four sides and raised to make the openings larger. Smoke was pouring out.

I went back into the house. "No need to pray," I said. "Gomez has taken care of it."

He came by the next morning in his truck and got out smiling.

"*Buenos días,*" he said. "Your fireplace—it is working all right?"

"It works fine," I said. "*Gracias.*"

"A miracle," he said.

I didn't mention the refrigerator. It had never worked from the beginning. Now it had given up freezing everything. It no longer worked at all. But one miracle at a time. For the moment, I was content with the miracle of the fireplace.

CHAPTER SEVENTEEN

Not long after the house was finished our younger son, Doug, married a Frenchwoman named Jacqueline Joyeux, and soon our daughter-in-law's mother came over from France on her first visit to America. She wanted to see our Baja house. Her daughter had described it romantically in her letters, and our warnings about the road would not dissuade Mme Joyeux from making the trip.

As it turned out, it was not Mme. Joyeux, after all, who was ill at ease. She seemed to fall at once into harmony with the pace and mood of Baja, though it would seem to have had nothing in common with St. Cyr, her native village near Tours.

It was our son who grew restless. "What's there to do on a Saturday night?" he asked after dinner.

It was our custom on Saturday nights, or any other nights, to read and listen to music on the radio from Tijuana, but I didn't think that was what he had in mind.

"We could go over to the port," I said, remembering what fun it had been the day the men were putting up the light.

"What do they have over there?"

"Well, they have an electric light, and beer, and somebody might be playing the guitar and singing."

On the other hand, I pointed out, it was two miles to

the port, and the road was perhaps too difficult, even for the indomitable Mme. Joyeux.

"That leaves Gomez's store," I said.

We got in the car and drove to the store. The light was on and Gomez was in, standing behind his counter with his hat pushed back. There was only one customer, a man solemnly drinking a beer. We said our greetings and I introduced Gomez to Mme. Joyeux, explaining that she was from France and spoke no English.

"*Ah, bon soir, madame,*" said Gomez, suddenly oozing charm. "*Parlez-vous Español?*"

I was astonished. When and where would Gomez have acquired any French? It was another of those flashes he occasionally gave of depths and experiences he ordinarily seemed reluctant to reveal.

"What is your pleasure?" he asked.

"*Cerveza,*" said my son, remembering the Spanish word. The women decided on a carbonated apple juice, highly recommended by Gomez. They sat on the wooden bench and drank it from the bottle with Gomez's dogs at their knees.

"*Señor* Smith?"

"Do you have a bottle of wine?"

"A bottle, *señor?*"

"Yes. We are having a night out. I will buy the bottle of wine, and you and I will drink it."

Gomez at once grasped the festive spirit of the evening. He produced a bottle of Santo Tomás red and set two glasses on the counter. He opened the wine and poured.

"To Madame Joyeux," I said, raising a glass. It was the first of several excellent toasts.

Unfortunately, the apple juice was finished before the wine. The dogs began to snap at each other and the women grew restive. We said *buenas noches* at last and drove back to the house in the dark.

I was up before the rest of the household the next morning and made some coffee and sat out on the porch with my binoculars to see what was happening on the bay.

The fishermen were already out, their wooden boats no more than straws on the sea. Near the rocks two men in a blue boat were diving in black wetsuits. A flock of pelicans flew by, too many to count. How odd that the pelican should look so comical when sitting on a rock, and so stately in flight. There was a white sloop moving out from the port under power, and then a white sail blew out and filled and the boat turned out toward the open sea.

In a while Denny got up and began to wonder about what to fix for breakfast. We had to consider our guests. "Do you think you could get us some fish?" she asked.

I swung the glasses around to examine the boats. Gomez had got an old eighteen-footer and painted it blue and was now in the fishing business. He didn't go out himself, but entrusted the boat to a fisherman named Chuy. I thought I saw them out beyond the seaweed.

"Maybe so," I said. "I'll go see."

I drove to the store. It was the old story. The man setting out in the morning to get the fish, his mate waiting beside the fire. Gomez was not at his counter, but I heard cooking sounds and smelled tortillas browning on the fire. In a moment he came out of the kitchen.

"*Buenos días,*" he said. "You are just in time for breakfast."

"I can't stay," I said. "They're all waiting breakfast on me. Do you have any fish?"

"No fish yet, *señor.* The boat is not back."

Through the door I saw a girl standing in the kitchen; a young woman. She was looking out the window toward the sea and patting a tortilla in her hands in the ancient way. I couldn't remember seeing her before.

"You have a new girl to help out?" I asked.

"Oh, yes. Pepe has got married. She is his wife."

I was oddly surprised. I had often wondered how two charming young men like Pepe and Sergio could be content to spend so many of their days at Bocana, away from the excitements and the nubile girls of Tijuana. The truth was, of course, that they were more often in Tijuana than here in Bocana. I had been very naïve to imagine them without sweethearts.

Mrs. Gomez appeared in the doorway. "Come in, Jack, have some hot tortillas."

"Thank you," I said. "I'd better hurry back."

"I have just made salsa," she said, knowing my weakness for her salsa.

I went into the kitchen and she introduced me to the bride. "This is Estela," she said. "Pepe's wife."

Estela Gomez said *buenos días* and went on patting tortillas. She was a very pretty girl, as demure on the surface as custom required; but I caught a flash of mischief in her eyes. I suspected that she and Delia Gomez had already formed a secret alliance against the male world.

Mrs. Gomez gave me a stack of tortillas and a bowl of salsa. Her salsa is superb; spicy and succulent and full of delayed and unexpected fires. You spread the salsa on the tortilla, which is hot and crisp but not too crisp to roll, and you roll it up and eat it, using your fingers. I was on my third tortilla when Gomez put a paper cup in front of me half-full of a clear liquid.

"So early?" I said.

"You don't wish to drink to the bride?"

"Of course."

"Besides," said Gomez, "it will make your morning happy."

He put half a lime and a salt shaker down beside the cup. I hoped I could remember the ritual. First the salt on the tongue, then the tequila, then a bite of the lime.

"To Pepe and Estela," I said, as the warmth began inside and spread outward like a slow explosion.

"It makes you happy?" said Gomez in a moment.

"I am very happy."

When I left Mrs. Gomez gave me a stack of tortillas in a paper napkin to take back to the others. "To make up for the fish," she said.

I walked outside with Gomez and told him my wife would be disappointed, as I was, that we hadn't been to the wedding.

"Nobody was invited," he said. "These kids, they just run off and get married. It is these modern times."

Pepe had gone the way of his generation and flouted tradition. It had been a civil ceremony in Tijuana, and Pepe had come home with his bride to the surprise of everyone.

But Gomez was soon enough very happy with his daughter-in-law, except for one shortcoming. Her father was a successful Tijuana businessman, and as a result of her having grown up in affluence, there was a gap in her education.

"She does not know how to make tortillas," said Gomez.

"But I see she is learning," I said.

"Oh, yes. Of course."

On the way back, I stopped to look at the new house. Gomez had said it would be finished in three months; my guess was closer to nine.

They were waiting when I got back to the house, sipping coffee and orange juice and looking out the window.

"You have the fish?" Denny asked.

"No. The boat wasn't back yet. But don't worry. I am very happy. I have just drunk a toast to Pepe's bride."

What more could a woman want than a mate who came home happy, and with news of a wedding?

She forgave me.

That summer we spent nearly every weekend, plus whatever time we could spare from our jobs, at Bocana. On the whole, the house worked well, and we adjusted to its minor inconveniences without complaint.

The problem of the refrigerator, however, was not soon overcome. We had been in the house a year before we solved it. On this one score, Gomez had failed us. He had tried, but the old Servel could not be made to perform. In vain he had looked for another Servel to take its place. But Servel had not manufactured a gas refrigerator in fifteen years, and the old ones were scarce in Baja. Even Luczynski had tinkered with the refrigerator, and given it up.

At last, in spring, after an exasperating year of living out of our cool can, we mounted an expedition one weekend from Los Angeles and attained the elusive victory. The operation, I must say, was brilliantly conceived and executed. Dalton went down a day early as advance man, to take in firewood, beer, and water. The rest of us rendezvoused at 0600 on a Saturday at our house in Los Angeles —our old friend Steve Baer, young Chris Baer, his son, Dick Wass, my wife, and I.

It was Baer who had hatched the plan months earlier. He was with the gas company in Los Angeles, and his friend

Wass was an executive who had come up through the ranks in the company, but hadn't carried a toolbox in years.

"If it can be fixed," Baer had told me, "Wass can fix it. Just get him the model number and the BTU. They should be inside the thing someplace."

What was most likely needed, Wass had thought, was a new orifice, to adapt the burner to butane. On my next trip to Bocana I had looked inside the box and found the pertinent data. The refrigerator had been made in 1941. It had been in service when Japan bombed Pearl Harbor. No wonder the price had been so high. It was a genuine antique.

With his connections in the gas industry, Wass had been able to scrounge the proper orifice, and we were in high spirits as we drove down the coast. But we men fell into a pensive spell as we passed the mothball fleet in San Diego Bay, those rows of gray warships, so powerfully nostalgic. It turned out we were all three veterans of the Pacific theater.

Baer had been a radioman in a mine sweeper, a homely old wood hull-type that never swept a mine in the entire war. The high point of the war for Baer had been when he radioed the ship's identity to a passing cruiser which had asked, "Are you the garbage scow?"

Wass had been a navy machinist's mate, never knowing that the skills he was learning under fire would serve him on this international mission a quarter of a century after V-J Day.

We reached the house in Baja just after 1200 hours. Wass got out of the car with his toolbox and went to work at once. He made an extensive examination. It wasn't simply a matter of installing the new orifice. Tubes and flues had to be blown out. Joints had to be secured.

Dalton came up from the beach with some seashells.

Gomez drove over from the store in his pickup with his dogs. We watched and waited. There were time-outs for rest, beer, and consultation. It was nearly 1700 when Wass lighted the burner, shut the door and said he had done all a human being could do. We must wait.

"What's the prognosis?" Baer asked.

"It's too early to say. It may be an hour, two hours, maybe three, before we know."

We decided to go ahead with the cocktail hour. At 2100 hours we opened the door and felt inside. It was noticeably colder, but not nearly cold enough. "I'm not optimistic," Wass said.

At 2300 the indications were good. There was a heart-warming coldness and a feel of moisture. We put the beer in and went to bed. There was nothing more to do but wait.

In the morning I was awakened by shouting.

"By God, it's ice!" It was Dalton.

We gathered in the kitchen. I pulled an ice tray. It was full of solid cubes. We looked at Wass.

"One final test," he said. He took a bottle of beer out of the refrigerator and opened it. He took a swallow. He sighed.

"The crisis is over," he said.

While the others were celebrating I made an entry in my log.

Sunday, April 7. Refrigerator fixed.

It was the most momentous entry since the day the toilet flushed.

Occasionally we had to be away from Bocana for long stretches. Though I can dismantle a tidy house in five minutes, I am very reluctant to leave one that is not tidy. Perhaps this comes from my maritime training. A ship must be scrubbed down and polished up before the first man goes ashore. A weekend house is like a ship. It must be ready to sail, so to speak, on a moment's notice.

It is our practice before we leave, therefore, to make the beds and stow all the dishes and lock the windows and put each piece of furniture in its proper place. It is reassuring, when we come back, to find everything just as we left it.

So I was vaguely uneasy one weekend when we opened up the house after an absence of two weeks. I didn't know what it was, but something was out of place; not much, but enough to disturb some pattern in my memory. It was the kind of feeling you might have in returning to a long-interrupted chess game, only to sense that your opponent has made some surreptitious move.

It was there in the living room, but I couldn't focus on it. I put it out of my mind and sat down to watch the sun set. It sets straight out in front of our windows, so close you think you can see it move. It is said that anywhere in the world, when the sun sets in the sea on a cloudless day, at the last instant, when the last bit of fire is quenched, there is a green flash on the horizon. It was just such a cloudless evening, and I hoped to witness this phenomenon from my window.

Once before, I thought I had seen it, but the flash is said to be of such brief duration that it is over before you are conscious of it. As a boy I had read about it in one of the romantic novels of Jules Verne. Recently I had borrowed the book from the library, to refresh my memory. The sky must be pure, Verne had said, and then the sun's last ray would not be red but green. "It will be green, but a most wonderful green, a green which no artist could ever obtain on his palette, a green of which neither the varied tints of vegetation nor the shades of the most limpid sea could ever produce the like. If there be green in Paradise, it cannot but be of this shade, which most surely is the true green of hope."

I sat in the new yellow reclining chair. I keep it in a corner near the fireplace, facing our front windows for the view of the sea, and with its back to a side window for reading in the daylight.

The sun was halfway gone. I kept my eye on it, trying to tell if I could really see it moving. It was strange. It seemed not to move, and yet every moment there was less of it to see. Suddenly the last sliver of fire was gone and then I saw, I swear, a flash of green.

"Fantastic!" I shouted. "I saw it!"

In my excitement I rocked back in the chair, stretching it into the full recline position, and in the same instant I heard the clink and tinkle of shattering glass.

I knew then what was wrong with the living room. Some fool had moved the yellow chair a foot or so closer to the side window.

In the morning I removed the aluminum frame with the broken pane and put it in the back seat of the car and drove it over to the store. That part of the road is very rough, and there were moments when I was glad the window was already broken. I hoped Gomez would take it into Ensenada on his next trip and have the glass replaced.

He was out in back of the store working on the old water truck. I was glad to see that the truck was parked by the well, though I knew of course that sometimes it was filled directly from the lagoon.

"*Buenos días,*" said Gomez.

"Buenos días," I said. "I have a broken window."

He frowned. "Someone has broken your window?"

"It was an accident. I did it myself."

He smiled. "Ah, *bueno.* That is good."

The hood of the truck was off and Gomez bent over to peer into the engine. He went in deeper—head, shoulders, and hat—probing with both arms. He had the usual gallery—a small boy, two fishermen, an American with a can of beer, and a local woman with a baby. Anywhere in Baja an open hood will draw a crowd. On the loneliest road they come out of the bushes, sometimes shepherd boys who know more about carburetors than mechanics in American garages.

I got out of the car and looked into the water truck's engine with the others. It looked like a piece of machinery you might expect to find half-buried in sand on an old World War II battlefield outside Tobruk.

Finally Gomez raised his head and shoulders from the greasy compartment of the engine, his hat miraculously still in place, and brought out an electric cable, about eighteen inches long and obviously frayed and corroded beyond salvage. He handed the cable to one of the fishermen, without a word, and turned to me.

We appraised my problem, which soon had Gomez's audience as absorbed as they had been with his. It was decided that I would take the window to Ensenada myself, thus expediting its repair. On the way back it could ride end-up in the back seat. Gomez got down on the ground on one knee and drew a map in the dirt. I was to go to the monument of Juarez, then turn left and go on two blocks. There, on my right, I would find the glazier's.

We had no sooner got the window in the car than the fisherman who had taken the bad cable reappeared suddenly with another cable. It wasn't a new one, I saw, but it looked serviceable. Where had he got it? Cannibalizing wrecks is the secret of auto life in Baja, but where was the wreck he had cannibalized? Prompted by a vague solicitude, I glanced at my own car, but saw with relief that the hood was still down.

Gomez's map was true. I found the glazier's. The girl at the counter was very beautiful; a dark saintly classic beauty. We smiled at each other through our language barrier. I pointed to the frame with its broken pane and raised my eyebrows. She nodded. She looked at her watch. She pursed voluptuous lips.

"*Dos horas,*" she said.

"Fine," I said. "Two hours."

I left the window and drove down to the Bahía de Todos Santos and out to the boathouse restaurant on the water. The tables were empty. It was not a day for American tourists. I sat by a misty window and ordered the abalone and a glass of Santo Tomás blanco.

Under a broken sky the bay had a soft metallic sheen, blown into a million coins by the wind. A hundred fishing boats lay on the water like dabs of paint. Pelicans perched on the rusted buoys and lined up along the gunwale of a shipwreck. There was a distant chorus of creaks and toots and cries; the sounds of a harbor at work.

When I returned to the glazier's the window was ready. The beautiful girl said the bill was five dollars. I paid it and made the window secure in the back seat and set out for Bocana. Between me and the store were ten miles of detour and eighteen more miles of dirt road through the valley. I drove with prudence and a prayer.

When I reached the store the window was still intact. I had only the final mile to go.

"I'll make it," I told Gomez. "I said a prayer."

"Don't worry," said Gomez. "I have my fingers crossed."

I don't know who was responsible, but I made it.

Shortly after the incident of the window, Denny went down to Bocana alone. I was working hard against a deadline and couldn't get away.

For me, it turned out to be one of those weekends when little things went wrong. I had been plagued of late by a series of minor accidents that seemed to happen mostly on weekends when she wasn't home. First, a greasy skillet caught fire on the electric range and burned out the hood. Then later, the living room draperies knocked over a brass floor lamp, shattering the globe. On both of these occasions my wife returned from the five-hundred-mile journey with no mishaps to report at all.

This time I hoped to break the jinx, if that was what it was. I would be especially careful. I was bogged down with work, and it seemed reasonable to expect that I could keep the house intact. The Devil did not find work for busy hands.

On Saturday morning I put the teakettle on to make some tea. It was a beauty, of Swedish make, white enameled steel covered with blue and yellow flowers. It had a good whistle, also, but somehow I neglected to stick the whistle on the spout. Sometime later, realizing that it hadn't whistled, I hurried into the kitchen to see what was wrong. The water had boiled away. The kettle was red. It was fused to the burner. I grabbed the handle and yanked it free, a mistake that had the result of lifting the red-hot coils of the burner and bending them permanently out of shape, and at the same time putting a hole in the kettle and burning my hand.

I sat down to think it over. There was nothing really wrong with me. I was merely the victim of an unlikely string of mishaps. My luck would turn. Meanwhile, why was it that Denny never broke anything? She sometimes left dishes stacked like the Tower of Pisa. She could not be made to respect the principle of potential energy. Yet nothing ever fell. She had a guardian angel.

If only, I prayed, she would break something on this trip—just a saucer, maybe; or a cheap little teacup—something to show her that accidents can happen to anyone.

I took the ruined teakettle down to the garage and dropped it in the trash. A plan had formed. I would simply go out and buy a new one exactly like it, and no one would be the wiser. I am not given to petty dishonesties, but I didn't want her to worry about my mind.

Unfortunately, the store where I'd bought the teakettle didn't have another one exactly like it. They had the same pattern, but only in a smaller size. I bought it anyway. She might not notice the difference, and even if she did I could point out that things often looked smaller when you'd been away. If she insisted, I'd simply tell her it was *her* mind that was going, not mine.

That night I went out to a banquet, one of the obligations that had kept me home, but as soon as I was home again I phoned one of my sons to see if his mother had called. I always like to be within reach if she has an emergency.

"Where've you been?" he said. He sounded calm, but there was an undercurrent of anxiety. "We've been trying to get you all evening."

"What is it?"

"Mother phoned."

So something was wrong. The nearest phone was more than an hour away from Bocana. She must have gone into Ensenada to phone. It would have had to be an emergency.

"What is it!"

"She broke her leg."

He had been at work and his wife had got the call from Ensenada. She is a physical therapist and had taken the facts with professional poise. Denny had fallen on the rocks in the tidepools. She knew she was hurt. She tried to stand, but there was too much pain in her right leg, and a crunch. Fortunately, the Millards had been with her, and two friends of theirs, one a doctor. The doctor had told her to stay off the leg.

There is a steep and narrow and treacherous flight of stairs cut into the seacliff. There was no way the others could help her up, so she had gone up the stairs backwards, on her seat, with the injured leg held out like the little finger of a lady drinking tea.

They had driven her to the hospital in Ensenada. The doctors had made X-rays and found a spiral break above the ankle, and had at once encased her leg in a cast.

"How long," I asked, "will she be in the cast?"

"At least six weeks."

I decided to wait until morning to drive down after her, so our younger son could go with me and bring back her car. But I didn't sleep well. I kept telling myself it wasn't my fault. All I had asked for was a broken saucer, or a teacup. I didn't expect her to break a leg.

CHAPTER EIGHTEEN

Fortunately, though she was to limp for several months, Denny was out of her cast in time for the wedding of Sergio Gomez.

Sergio was to be married at four o'clock on a Saturday afternoon in Nuestra Señora de Carmen, the Gomez's neighborhood church in Tijuana. We drove down to the border and left our car on the American side, knowing we might never find Nuestra Señora de Carmen in the maze of Tijuana's back streets.

As many Americans do, we walked across the border, through Mexican customs, and caught a Mexican taxi, asking the driver to take us to the Hotel Caesar. We had allowed ourselves time for lunch before the wedding.

We lunched at Caesar's on seafood salad, with white wine, and caught another of the cabs which in Tijuana are as proliferous as they are scarce in Los Angeles.

"Do you know Nuestra Señora de Carmen?" I asked the driver.

He looked up at us with mild surprise, as if wondering why the American tourists would be going to a little Mexican church on a Saturday afternoon.

"We're going to a wedding," I explained.

His face lit up. *"Sí, sí!"* he said, turning to open the

door. He would be only too happy to drive us to such a happy event.

Nuestra Señora de Carmen was a small new church of modern design, with abstract stained glass windows and a streamlined Madonna. It was centuries removed from the big Spanish colonial cathedral at the heart of town.

We waited on the steps, watching as the guests arrived, and the members of the wedding. We saw Marisa among the bridesmaids, all very pretty and vivid in their billowing blue dresses.

"Look at that woman in black," I said. "She has to be one of Delia's sisters." Mrs. Gomez, I remembered hearing her say, was from a family of four girls.

The woman had the sculptured face and bronze skin of Mrs. Gomez, and the same half-smile and mischievous eyes. She was more urban, though, with her flawless coiffure, her false eyelashes, and her touch of lipstick. Her dress was black, but short and chic.

"Yes," my wife said. "It's astonishing, the resemblance."

I searched the growing crowd for Gomez. He was not in sight. At four o'clock a white Cadillac drew up before the church and Sergio stepped out in a mod tuxedo with a ruffled shirt. He was a handsome young man, I realized, as lean, quick and lithe as a bullfighter; and he was very nervous. We caught him for a moment at the door.

"Where's your father?" I asked. "We haven't seen him."

He shook his head. "My father is busy with the details of the reception. All morning he is too busy to get dressed for the wedding. He is driving my mother crazy."

"Where's Pepe?"

"He is at Bocana, watching the store."

It was time for the wedding. The guests were filing in to take their seats. At the last moment the woman in black went in and sat next to another woman in black, who also bore a striking resemblance to Mrs. Gomez. Another sister, I assumed.

"They look like they're in mourning," I said.

"Yes, that's it, of course."

Delia's mother had died several months ago, and Mrs. Gomez and her sisters would wear black in public for a year, even at her son's wedding. In Mexico, mourning is a serious obligation.

Suddenly the first woman in black looked our way and smiled at us from across the church.

"That's not Delia's sister!" Denny exclaimed. "It's *Delia!*"

It had come to me at the same instant. We had never before seen Mrs. Gomez away from Bocana, where her unvarying costume had been a shirt or sweater, slacks, and an apron. We had not been prepared to believe her as the soignée woman who now smiled so knowingly at us.

Suddenly the bride appeared in her cocoon of white. She was a mystery to us behind her veil. We had never seen her at Bocana, as we had never seen Pepe's fiancée before his marriage, perhaps because the conventions of their society would not have permitted such a sojourn.

The betrothed couple turned to face the altar. It was just then that a familiar figure in a dark suit came silently down the far aisle and slipped into the pew beside Delia Gomez.

"Thank God," I whispered. "He's here."

The priest spoke in Spanish and we could not follow his words, but his voice was grave and stern as he admonished the couple who knelt before him.

When the ceremony was over Sergio lifted the veil from his bride's face and kissed her with a resolution and vigor that amounted almost to abandon. It was the longest nuptial kiss I had ever seen.

They walked down the aisle toward the sunlight pouring through the open door and I saw that she was beautiful; radiant and vivacious as a bride should be, with large laughing eyes and an ivory skin that seemed lighted from within.

They stepped into the sunshine and a shower of rice and stood trapped as friends surged forward to congratulate the bridegroom and kiss the bride. Unfortunately, Sergio's attention was turned away as I approached, and he failed to introduce me as I closed in on the bride. I realized too late that she might not welcome a kiss from a man she had never seen before. I was already committed. Her eyes widened and she recoiled involuntarily, then stood her ground and braved it out, as I kissed her awkwardly on the cheek.

I shuffled on, mumbling something about happiness, and in a moment the newlyweds broke away and ran down the steps and were carried off in the white Cadillac.

We found Romulo and Delia Gomez among the crowd of friends. Gomez explained his tardiness. He had gone by the restaurant to make sure there was plenty of wine and tequila for the reception.

"Oh!" said Mrs. Gomez, "I was so angry!"

"You are coming to the reception, of course?" said Gomez.

It was held in a restaurant on Agua Caliente boulevard not far from the church. The arrangements had been elaborate. There were settings for a hundred guests at two long tables placed conveniently beside the dancefloor. It was not an affair of limp canapes and weak drinks, but a feast. There were toasts to the bride and bridegroom. Flashbulbs flared as they cut the cake. A band of mariachi appeared, half a dozen of them, in their gray uniforms with black trim and silver spangles. I couldn't understand the words, except for the *"amors"* and *"corazons,"* but the mariachi music speaks for itself. It is comical and sad and passionate; the cornet sobs of young love unrequited, and of youth and homelands far away.

Suddenly the music grew soft; the horns fell silent, and there was nothing but a violin and a lightly strummed guitar. Then a man began to sing in a voice strangely different from those of the mariachi. It was a mature voice, but sweet. Its ardor was restrained, its sadness mellowed. It was a marvelously fluid voice, falling on the notes of the violin and guitar like moonlight on windblown leaves.

> *Piedad, piedad, para el que sufre.*
> *Piedad, piedad, para el que llora . . .*

"My God!" I whispered in Denny's ear. "It's Romulo!"

Then he was singing in English, and that familiar accent, so elusive, softened the banal English words and made them poignant.

> *Tonight, tonight, we live forever,*
> *Tonight, tonight, will vanish never.*
> *Thousands of stars are hanging up in their places.*
> *This is the night for love and sweet embraces.*
> *The moon is bright, the breeze is tender;*
> *The scene is set for sweet surrender . . .*

When he finished there were tears in Denny's eyes; in mine too, but it might have been the tequila.

"Well, at last we know what he is," I said. "Whatever else he may be, he's an artist."

Sergio was tending the store when we saw him next.

"The honeymoon is over?" I asked.

"Oh, no, this is our honeymoon. Lilia is here with me. Pepe is here too."

"And Estela?"

"Of course. She is with Pepe. We are all on our honeymoon."

He opened the gate of the counter and led us into the kitchen. It was obvious that the brothers were no longer bachelors. The kitchen was in order. Estela was scouring pots and skillets at the sink and Lilia was chopping vegetables, for salsa, I supposed. We all said *buenos días*.

"I am the man who frightened you at the wedding," I said to Lilia, reminding her of the kiss.

She blushed and laughed. *"Sí, señor,"* she said. "I remember."

I had a tequila with Sergio and we went back out front. "The kitchen looks much better," I told him, "than it used to when you and Pepe were bachelors."

"Oh, yes. Of course. Everything is better."

"It was a fine reception," I said.

"Gracias. I am glad you came."

"I had no idea your father could sing like that," I said. "We were astounded. He once had a band, I believe he told us."

"My father sang with the first mariachi to play on the radio in Mexico City."

"He never sings anymore?"

Sergio shrugged. "You know. He is a busy man."

We drove to the house, wondering if the chance to hear Gomez sing the songs of his youth would ever come again.

"Oh, well, there's one more wedding to go," Denny said, and I knew she was thinking of Marisa.

The next morning I walked to the store to see if there was any fish.

"No, there is no fish," said Sergio. "You want to catch some fish?"

I hadn't thought of catching the fish myself. "You're going fishing?" I said.

"Why not? Chuy has just come in with the boat."

Chuy was Gomez's new handyman and fisherman. Like Gomez, he could do anything, though not, perhaps, with the same uncanny skill. He had a wife and five children in the village of Santo Tomás, and was always willing to give honest work for an honest dollar. He had gone out that morning with an American customer, but the American had drunk too much the night before, and was soon too sick to care about fishing.

"Chuy had to bring him back early," Sergio said. "He caught no fish. He is ready to go out again."

"How long would we be gone?"

"Maybe an hour."

I couldn't phone my wife, but I didn't think she'd miss me for an hour. I had left her working in the yard.

"I have no fishing tackle," I said.

"Don't worry. Chuy will furnish everything."

"It's probably cold out on the water. I don't have a jacket."

"No problem. We'll find you one."

Five minutes later, my objections depleted, I found myself in a weatherbeaten eighteen-foot wooden boat with Sergio and Pepe and their brides and a lad named Oscar. Chuy shoved us far enough into the surf to get his outboard motor down, then jumped in, making seven of us.

It was more of a lark than a fishing trip. I am not unreasonably afraid of water, but I was uneasy as we bobbed out over the waves toward the open sea. I knew the boat was overloaded, but it seemed a nice day, and it was obvious that Chuy was a boatsman. He stood at the oars, working us clear of the shoals and rocks, then took the oars in and yanked the outboard to life. The sky was blue, the sea was calm. I was soon serene.

We rounded a point and turned out into the bay. From a half mile out I saw Denny working in the yard. She was wearing a white denim pantsuit that stood out sharply against the brown hills. I waved my arms wildly; she never looked up. It occurred to me that we might be out longer than Sergio thought, and that she would begin to worry, not knowing where I was.

We moved out to sea and skirted Punta Santo Tomás and cruised up the coast toward Soledad Bay. A seal swam toward our prow but Pepe drove him off with a well-aimed Coke bottle, shouting what I assumed were Spanish curses.

"He would steal our fish," Pepe explained to me.

As we passed Seal Rock the old bull raised his head to scout us. He sounded no alarm to his harem. We were no immediate threat.

Chuy eased the boat into a clearing in a forest of sea-weed and tied the boat to one of the thick floating branches. He passed out poles and baited our hooks with anchovies, and soon all hands were fishing.

Not two minutes passed before I felt a tension on my line and then a light jolt. It was a strike. My pulse raced as the pole jumped in my hands and the fish's struggle became ripples of feeling in my arms. I reeled him in carefully, and he breached the surface, flashing and flopping, a glistening deep pink. He was twenty inches long, I guessed, as Chuy reached out to fetch him into the boat. At that moment the fish wriggled free and dropped into the water. I watched him go, smaller and smaller and darker and darker as he sank, vanishing like a sunset.

Later I caught a smaller cod, as a consolation, but it was no match for the one that got away.

We had been out two hours when the sky turned mean and the sea began to heave. Chuy told us to ship our poles. He rearranged us in the boat. It was time to run. We had waited too long.

As we turned the point again and crossed the bay I saw that Denny was still at work in the yard. I was disappointed, not to say annoyed. I thought that by now she would have wondered what had become of me and driven over to Bocana to find out. Not finding anyone there, she would naturally have been puzzled, if not worried half-crazy.

We beached in a dangerously heavy surf, with the brides screaming and the men shouting, half in anxiety and half in exuberance. Three times as we wallowed in shallow water, we had to turn back into the surf and ride up over a great breaker to avoid a certain breaching. Each time the wave rushed toward us, towering ten feet above our prow. The boat seemed to stand on its stern as it slid up to the crest; then the wave lifted the stern and the bow came down with a smack like a cannon shot. Lilia, on the seat beside me, screamed and threw her arms around me. I realized later that we would no longer feel awkward about the wedding kiss. We had shared a common peril. We were friends.

Chuy cleaned my little fish on the beach and I got a plastic bag from the store to take it home in. Sergio offered me a shot of tequila, which I could have used, but I knew I ought to hurry back to the house.

"My wife will be out of her mind," I told him.

When I walked up she was still in the yard, hacking at the earth with a hoe.

"Hi," she said, not looking up.

"Weren't you worried?"

"No. I thought you probably stayed at the store for lunch, with two young women to do the cooking."

"I went fishing and caught a fish."

"Good."

"We stayed out too long. The ocean got rough and it was very touch and go getting back."

"Sounds exciting. How do you like the little cactus I transplanted?"

Soon after that the confrontation I had dreaded finally came. I met my wife's rattlesnake. If I failed to act with compassion in this emergency, as some of our sentimental acquaintances later argued, at least I acted with dispatch.

We couldn't be certain, of course, that it was the same snake she had encountered earlier. But it fit the description. In any case, the snake's identity had no bearing on the moral issues.

I had been disappointed in her for letting the first snake get away. I was afraid he would be back. But I saw

her point. It takes emotional and physical energy to kill a
snake, and one must not falter. Being alone, without any
experience with snakes, without help in case of a mishap,
she had acted wisely enough.

I was right, however, about the snake coming back.

Denny was alone this time, too. I had gone over to the
store to get a tank of butane and left her digging up
tumbleweeds in front of the house. When I got back she
came in, pale and much too calm.

"What is it?"

"I had another encounter."

"Rattlesnake?"

"I don't know. He may have had stripes."

"If he had stripes he wasn't a rattlesnake."

"I think he had a rattle."

She had lifted up a giant tumbleweed and seen the
snake crawling away from her, under another weed. I have
always had a great respect for rattlesnakes, and am inclined to let them go their way. But this one was too close.
I got the hoe and we went outside and she showed me
where. I probed under the weed with the hoe and saw the
snake move. He was not striped. He had the head of a pit
viper, and he had three rattles. I stepped back, planted
myself firmly, raised the hoe and brought it down in one
quick careful stroke.

The moralists, the ecologists, and the nature lovers
who live fourteen stories up in their urban concrete tow-
ers may protest that a rattlesnake is one of God's creatures, too, and entitled to his own half-acre. They may
even say that the rattlesnake was there first, and I was the
intruder. I say none of us lives on ground that was not
once upon a time inhabited by reptiles.

That afternoon Denny drove over to the port to see if

she could buy some fish. There are always two or three fishermen in by that time with a fresh catch. She came back instead with two live lobsters in a cardboard box.

"Look what I have," she said, lifting one up by the feelers, or whatever they are.

"How interesting," I said. So far as I knew, she had never before dealt with a live lobster, and I guessed that she felt rather as Delia Gomez did about popping one into a pot of boiling water.

I went back to my book. I was reading *Cmdr. Prince; USN*, James Bassett's novel about a navy officer, a kind of Lord Jim and Captain Ahab, who must kill his nemesis to exorcise his own fear of cowardice. At one level of consciousness I could hear her going about her task. The big pot wrestled out of the cupboard. Running water. Pot on stove. Match. Gas flame hissing. In a while boiling water.

"Well," she said at last, "here goes."

Later she shelled the lobsters and chilled the meat and made a salad to go with our dinner of fresh rock cod. I felt quite pleased with myself and sensed that she was just as pleased with herself.

Later, when we told Pepe about the rattlesnake, he said that where you find one you will find another, probably a bigger one, fit to be tied over the loss of its mate.

I decided to let my wife deal with the next one. The separation of roles was all right up to a point.

CHAPTER NINETEEN

Since my wife's accident we have not worried as much about what might happen as we used to. We have had a broken leg and survived it, and there seems to be no point in worrying about snakes and mice and blowouts, and whether there will be water in the pipes or not, or even where it comes from.

Our friends still worry. They worry that the house is too far away, or too isolated, or, at the very least, too inconvenient, and, indeed, there is reason for anxiety on all these counts, especially since the oil shortage ended the American fantasy of unlimited fuel. They worry also about our lease, and they worry about rattlesnakes and scorpions and sharks and stingrays.

To tell the truth, I was worried about stingrays myself, for a while. To say the least for a snake, you meet him in your element, on terra firma, in the open air, and you can hear him rattle before he strikes. But when we first came to Bocana, Gomez had the carcass of a stingray hanging in his store, and at night in the glow of the single overhead lamp, which seems to cast more shadows than light, it was not an agreeable sight. I once asked Gomez about the likelihood of meeting such a thing in the bay. The stingray, or devilfish, as it is understandably called, is known to venture into the shallows and lie flat on the sand, and if he is stepped on, his tail whips up, plunging his poison barb into the hapless wader's ankle.

"Don't worry," Gomez said. "He does not come into this bay, that fish. The water is too cold."

"Well, what about that one?" I asked, indicating the monster on the wall.

"Ah, that little fish," said Gomez, "he did not know the rules. He came into the bay and he froze himself to death."

I suppose some changes will come to our bay. Gomez would like to build a few more houses, and we would not mind a few more neighbors. The road to La Paz is finished, and undoubtedly it will cause Americans to discover the forgotten peninsula. But we are eighteen hard miles off the highway, and perhaps most of them will ignore our turnoff in their hurry to go on to the splendid deserts and seascapes that lie ahead.

Men whose names we don't know are still at work on new roads to Puerto Santo Tomás and beyond, to new developments that still exist only on paper. Perhaps they will prosper. Or perhaps all their energy and zeal and money will merely blow away, like the smoke from our fireplace, and their projects, like so many before them, will vanish in the Baja sand.

The Schmidt house is finished at last, and it is truly a mansion. It is eighty feet across the front, and the living room–kitchen is fifty feet wide and thirty-five feet deep. At the center of this great space stands the sturdy pillar that holds up the main beam of the roof. It reminds Schmidt of his innocence in failing to foresee its need when he designed the house. But a pretty tile-covered bench has been built around the base of the pillar, giving some aesthetic value to what was purely functional.

As it turned out, the unforeseen pillar at the center of the living room was not the most distressing of the trials that beset the Schmidts. They had intended all their interior woodwork to be stained walnut, even the rafters, beams, and ceiling. But something went irreversibly awry. Schmidt had brought down several aerosol cans of a product called Derusto, and left them with Salvador, the carpenter, instructing him to spray all the wrought iron fixtures in the house. The purpose of Derusto is to protect iron from rust, and its color is black.

Salvador, of course, is a better carpenter than he is a painter, and sometimes he drinks a little, and sometimes has romantic notions. Whatever the reason, Salvador used the Derusto to spray the kitchen cabinets, which now are all quite black, their beautiful walnut grain beyond recall. The Schmidts were dismayed, but Schmidt, as usual, is philosophical about it. As he says, at least the cabinets will never rust.

There is also the difficulty with the bathtub, Salvador being a better carpenter than he is a tub man, too. When he built the bathtub, he was carried away, evidently, by the grand proportions of the house. The tub is so big that it could not be filled, according to Schmidt, by all the hot water in Baja.

Also, Salvador did not think to make the bottom of the tub slant slightly toward the drain, so the water would drain out. As a carpenter, it is Salvador's credo that all things should be level. Thus, he tried to make the bottom of the bathtub level, but even in this he failed. What he achieved, in fact, was a bottom that slants, not toward, but

away from the drain, so that when the Schmidts finish
taking baths they must stand up in the tub and squeegee
the water up toward the drain. It is Schmidt's contention
that the only way this quirk will ever be corrected is by the
repeal of the law of gravity, which is beyond even the
capacities of Gomez.

Nonetheless, the Schmidts love their house and are
quite content.

Sergio's bride is expecting, and it was the prospect of this
new responsibility, I suppose, that moved him to embark
on the ill-fated pig-raising venture with Millard.

We might never have heard the story if I hadn't gone
into the store one day and noticed an unusual aroma
coming from the kitchen. It was familiar enough—sweet
and succulent, but not an aroma I could associate with
Delia Gomez's cuisine.

"We are cooking a little pig," said Gomez.

"A pig?" I said. There seemed hardly room enough in
Delia's kitchen for such a formidable undertaking. But
Delia, it turned out, wasn't doing the cooking. She wanted
no part of it. The pig was being cooked by Isabel, an old
woman who lives up the road in an adobe house and had
been called in by Gomez for this extraordinary culinary
project.

"It is a long story," Gomez said. "Would you like a
beer?"

Sergio had wanted to widen his economic horizons.
He is an enterprising young man in any case, and his
marriage had naturally heightened his ambition. Even
during his honeymoon he had acquired some plywood
and built a new counter for the store and added some

shelves to increase its capacity. But he hungered for something with a growth factor, as Schmidt might have put it; an economic future.

"So he and Millard," said Gomez, "they formed a corporation."

"A corporation?"

"Yes, they formed a corporation to raise pigs."

Millard had provided the capital for the purchase of a male and a female, from Abel, up in the valley. Sergio's contribution had been the construction of a plywood pigpen directly behind the store, at the edge of the lagoon.

I was surprised at Millard's participation in such an unlikely business, considering his background as an executive in the canned food industry. A two-pig operation hardly seemed his kind of challenge. But perhaps he missed the arena of private enterprise.

"What did your wife think of the idea," I asked, "having a pig farm right outside her kitchen window?"

"She was against it," said Gomez.

He had warned the two officers of the corporation that the pigs would have to be well fed or they would root their way under the pen and get out, and then there was a danger that one of Gomez's dogs would do them in.

"I told them," he said, "they must bring the little pigs out and show them to the dogs. Let the dogs sniff around and get acquainted. Those dogs, they never saw a pig before."

"What were they planning to feed the pigs?" I asked.

"Scraps from the table, of course," said Gomez.

That seemed an unpromising plan. There would be few scraps. Mrs. Gomez was not a wasteful cook; nor were those who had the luck to sit at her table likely to leave much on their plates. As for Gordon and Opal Millard, they lived alone, and were spare eaters. Their leftovers would hardly be more than hors d'oeuvres for two hungry pigs.

"What happened?"

"Millard," said Gomez, "he would come over after lunch with this little handful of food for the pigs. You know—sandwiches?"

"Sandwiches?"

Gomez demonstrated, unable to conceal his delight at the picture of Millard tippy-toeing down to the pigpen with a handful of dainty leftovers. I fell hysterically against the counter.

"What finally happened?" I said at last.

Gomez shrugged. "When nobody was here, the little pigs they were hungry, so they dig their way under the fence and escape. The dogs got one, of course. Percy, they have not found him yet."

"Percy?"

"That is the name of the pig they have not found."

"And the one the dogs got?"

Gomez nodded toward the kitchen. "He is in there."

"What is the corporation going to do now?" I asked.

"Well," said Gomez, "if they find Percy, Millard is going to buy another female, and they will try again. This time maybe they will follow my advice. How about you? Would you like to join the corporation?"

"No, thanks," I said. "I don't have much of a head for business."

On the other hand, I might go in. If nothing else, it ought to be an excellent tax shelter. I must ask Schmidt for advice.

Bocana prospers, at its own pace. The foundation trenches are dug for a new house, which will stand between the Millard place and Luczynski's, and the men are filling them with stones. It will take time. Gomez is building the house for a young couple named Hughes, and at the moment that is all we know of them. Someday the house will be finished and they will join our colony.

The copper mine remains inoperative and the pebbles are still on the beach, but it may not always be so. Gomez hopes to buy a pump so he can pump water to the reservoir from his well, or the lagoon, and not have to make so many trips with the old water truck. Then he will have more water to build more houses.

Now that we know his secret, he sometimes comes to our house for dinner with his wife and his guitar and sings for us by candlelight. We are enchanted, and Delia Gomez seems enchanted, too, but there is always that humor in her eyes. Once when he was courting her in Tijuana, she says, he brought an entire mariachi band to her window and sang for an hour before he found out she wasn't home.

One day when I was climbing over the lava rocks in the surf below our house I happened to look up and a geological phenomenon caught my eye. The cliff below our house is perhaps forty feet high, and the house stands back a hundred feet or so from its edge. Halfway up its face the cliff is volcanic, a rock so hard that even the sea would make little progress against it in a thousand years. Above that, though, I noticed that the earth looked soft and chalky, and here and there it had been wrinkled by erosion. The surf could never reach that high. So it must be that the runoff from the rain was eating into the cliff from the top. Year by year it was inching closer to the house. Every storm must carve it deeper. Inexorably it advanced on our vain little pile of bricks. How soon, I wondered, would the whole house fall? It looked to me like about two hundred years.

That night at the store I told Gomez about this unrelenting peril. "Someday, Romulo," I said, "our mansion is going to slide right into the Pacific Ocean."

"Oh, yes," he said. "Of course. Someday. But not too soon. Five hundred years from now, Jack, you will still be living in that house."

"Maybe so," I said. "But isn't there something we can do about it now?"

"Well," said Gomez, "would you like to try a little tequila?"

Jack Smith is a newspaper reporter, magazine writer, and, for the past fifteen years, he has been a daily columnist for the *Los Angeles Times*. Before joining the *Times* in 1953, he worked on several newspapers, including the *Honolulu Advertiser*, the *Los Angeles Daily News*, and the *Los Angeles Herald-Express*. During World War II he joined the U.S. Marine Corps, serving two years as a combat correspondent. He has published six books and his articles have appeared in *Reader's Digest, The Saturday Evening Post, Holiday, McCall's, Travel & Leisure, Los Angeles,* and *Westways*. He and his wife, Denise, live in Los Angeles and Baja California.